All and Everything in diagrams

All & Everything in Diagrams

Organic Whole of the entire esoteric knowledge

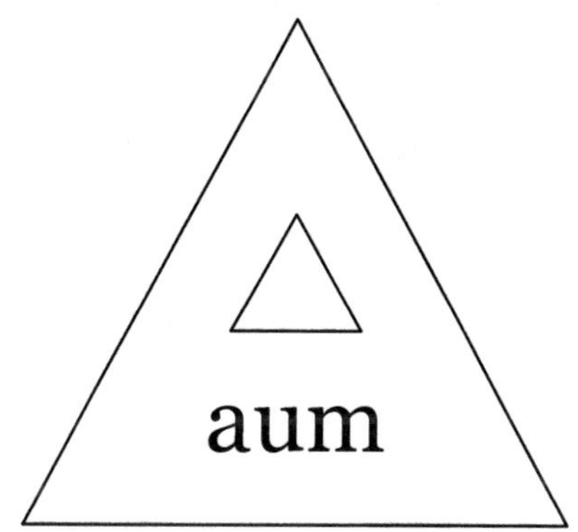

The Law of Three,

Ray of Creation, Material Devolution,

Psychological Evolution, States of Consciousness,

Basic Processes (Karmas) & Chief-Features (Vikarmas),

Body-Types, Health-Prakriti, Centre of Gravity,

Astronomy, the Law of Seven and

Process of Multiplicity from the basic Unity.

Mohan Vaishnav

Narrow Gate Press
London MMXIII

Published by Narrow Gate Press,
7 Riverside Drive, Richmond TW10 7QA, England
www.ngp.co

ISBN: 978-0-9565497-5-4

Dedication

Luckily thy fragrance was with me quite long,
As mom's touch to babe it's sweetened my heart;
The Nectar was thy love, which washed all wrong;
It's past belief: what efforts on my part?

That bloom of bliss waned with a trip of time;
Like a musk deer, I searched – "Where it went?"
I tried path this and that but missed thy rhyme;
Some cheer here and there, but, all like home on rent.

By thy shine on my Soul the dark did clear,
When I stayed heedful like a pregnant girl
And dropped all Hows and Buts. Now, have no fear.
Lo, thou'rt here, behind the veil of brain-whirl!

Brings joyous tears this eye-giving meet;
In gratitude, I lay these lines at thy feet.

Acknowledgements

I am grateful to Dr Martin Dace, who himself is a poet, painter, writer, reviewer, fellow journeyman, considerate fellow friend and the publisher of this book, for his patient reading of its various drafts & for his valuable suggestions, particularly the suggestion to incorporate explanatory notes for most of the terms used in this book to make the book more useful and read-worthy even for people who are not familiar with this terminology, and for his patient, friendly & loving support throughout the process.

I am grateful to Pujya Shri Anandswarup Swami of Akshardham, Gandhinagar, India for his loving and encouraging appreciations since the beginning.

I am grateful to my wife Urmi and my family for giving me loving, undisturbed and conducive atmosphere throughout the process.

I am also thankful to Article Trainees of my professional firm, particularly Nidhi Bhavsar, Piyush Nakrani & Arpit Jain for respectfully & accurately carrying almost entire professional burden of the firm during this period giving me undisturbed free time and conducive atmosphere for thinking and writing this book.

I am also thankful to Arjun Odedra of M/s. Ram Computers, Ahmedabad for carefully & untiringly composing complex Diagrams.

M.V

Contents

Publisher's foreword

This book is an ambitious attempt to relate the Fourth Way teaching of Gurdjieff, Ouspensky and Rodney Collin to the Sanskrit terminology of the Hindu tradition, and to create an organic synthesis of the whole of esoteric knowledge.

In this book Mohan Vaishnav presents us with some quite intricate tables, depicting possible levels of being and the workings of spiritual laws. All previous cultures have recognised levels of existence of which our unexamined life is almost the lowest. Mohan catalogues these other, higher levels according to his deep understanding of the Hindu and Fourth Way traditions.

How do we know that these other levels exist?

Some will say, 'This is all there is.' In a sense they are right. But it depends on what their *this* encompasses. There is *this*, a state of identification where we become fixated on some desire or feeling of resentment which takes us over and blinds us to what is around us.

> *There are demon-haunted worlds, regions of utter darkness* – Isa Upanishad.

Then there is *this*, the activity of chattering mind (*Manas* in Sanskrit).

And there is *this*, the wordless present. Already we can know, even such as we are, that less subjective states are possible if we make the right efforts.

Waking is better than dreaming, and there are less clouded states of awareness potentially available to us, clearer than the so-called waking state.

As Mohan says, "We all have, at some point of time, experienced that when our ordinary mind is not thinking, not chattering inside, and is wordless, and our heart is not resenting and judging anything and is just standing still in aliveness, for us it is moments of bliss."

> *Raise the stone, and there you will find me; cleave the wood, and there I am.* – Gospel of Thomas, *Saying 77*.

Some of this material may pass us by completely or have no use for us at the moment. Some of the proposed connections and correspondences may be questioned or be beyond our present level of understanding. Mechanically, we tend to reject as worthless what we do not understand. Yet the conjunction of two previously separate ideas can on occasion illuminate something for us and put a moment of fire into our work. In addition, the immense sense of scale in the diagrams, showing not just one but many higher worlds closer and closer to the Absolute, reminds us that we are all just at the beginning.

For me at any rate, and perhaps for others too, the most useful part is the section beginning with the heading *Practical work on Sattva, Rajasa and Tamasa*, and even more so the clarification of Patanjali's system from the *Yoga Sutras* in easily understandable Fourth Way terms, reminding us of what is possible in a way that relates to our own experience.

The diagrams themselves exist in this our lower realm, the realm where not only thinking, speech and books but also movement, eating and drinking, dancing, singing and all the ordinary emotions live. At the heart of any true religion or spiritual system is something more that cannot be said. The philosopher Ludwig Wittgenstein wrote, 'Whereof one cannot speak, thereof one must be silent' (*Tractatus* 7). So all any artist, dancer, lover or writer can do with what cannot be said is to offer signposts, or point.

We cannot eat, dance, sing or talk our way out of our subjectivity, as Ouspensky said, but we can remember our way out. And if a diagram or a set of words can act as a reminder and an inspiration then that is its value.

One more thing should be added. It must be rare indeed that anyone can find their way out on their own, however many books they read and however many things they attempt. At some point the help of those who know becomes necessary.

Martin Dace
Richmond upon Thames, England 2013

Introduction

Understanding is a result of connecting things with the whole. If one does not have idea of the whole, how can one connect, and how understanding would becomes possible? Without connecting part's place and significance to the entire scheme of the whole, it would be like studying veins of a leaf in minute detail without knowing anything about the tree. As Rodney Collin says: "Those who have been able to assimilate all the teaching into one coherent mental picture are very lucky— for whole it is, and in that lies its miraculous power".

This work is a result of putting on paper various esoteric ideas, which are already available in fragments in various esoteric traditions and writings. Basically, it is an attempt to structure the ***organic whole*** of the entire body of esoteric knowledge by applying the law of scale & relativity, and connecting important ideas according to their exact place and significance in that organic whole, in a coherent manner, in simple Diagrams, to make its right discerning easier.

In an attempt not to load it with lengthy theory, it is intentionally presented in simple diagrams and in brief explanatory notes, so that the grasp of the ***Picture of the Whole & Parts*** enter directly into our that *part*, which understands things without words (e.g. when one sees the symbol + one understands entire significance of + without words). Then, one may explore the minute details of a particular idea, keeping in view its relative place in that whole, in such a way that any possibility of lopsidedness or bias can be minimized. This results into and represents a higher method of learning.

In explanatory notes, wherever possible, the entire concept has been presented in one or few long sentences to evoke directed & controlled attention, and in short paragraphs to make its discerning easier.

In the process of exploring oneself, it came about slowly over a period of more than seven years, as the significance and relative place of various ideas unfolded. This exercise is an attempt to make it as an essential clue, a roadmap, and overall yardstick for understanding, applying and verifying the esoteric knowledge in one's own spiritual evolution. It needs to be rightly understood; deeply felt; and practically applied and explored, in non-identified way, in one's personal work (*sadhana*).

For right and scientific understanding of higher esoteric ideas, the searchlight of the Law of Three, and the Principle of Scale & Relativity, as expounded by G. I. Gurdjieff, P. D. Ouspensky and Rodney Collin in the 4th Way books namely, *In the Search of the Miraculous, The 4th Way* and *The Theory of Celestial Influence* is of a great help.

Keeping this searchlight in mind, one may explore the writing of Buddha; the higher understanding of human psyche, and the literary beauty & *meaning-density* of words reflected in works of William Shakespeare, particularly in his Sonnets; the philokalia; Tao Te Ching of Laotzu; Jainism in general and as it is expounded in works of Dada Bhagwan in particular; Sufism in general and as it is reflected in poetry of Rumi, Hafiz & Kabir in particular; *PatanjaliYogaSutras;* the *Upnisadas*, particularly the *Mandukya Upnisad*; the Bhagwad Geeta; and Bhagwan Swaminarayana's *Vachnamrits*, particularly *Vachnamrit* of *Gadhada* - I (12 & 46) & *Vachnamrit* of *Bhugol-Khagol*. However, there is no limit to the esoteric exploration. In all esoteric traditions and esoteric rituals there lie invaluable treasures, if approached in a right manner.

Understanding of rightly blending together fundamentals of the Law of Three of the 4th Way and Law of *TRIGUNA* (*Satva-Rajas-Tamas*) of Hindu Texts; and the understanding of relativity of *Tathata* of Buddhism; *Kaivalya* of Jainism; *Tao* of Laotzu; *Fana* of Sufism; and principles of *AksharBrahm* & *Purushottama* of the Bhagwad Geeta is a blessing & grace.

These esoteric ideas are already there as written & told in then prevailing ways. But in modern scientific way, perhaps, such *whole-structuring* attempt is being made for the first time. It is like, as William Shakespeare says:

> *"For as the sun is daily new and old,*
> *So is my love still telling what is told."*

2013
Ahmedabad, India

Mohan Vaishnav
mohan.vaishnav@gmail.com

About the diagrams

Here the basic attempt is to structure the ***organic whole*** of the entire body of esoteric knowledge by placing in hierarchical order almost all significant esoteric ideas in various Diagrams in pictorial & tabular way, in the form which that ideas assume at various cosmos levels (that is, at various levels of being).

For example, at *World 6* cosmos level, the *Satva,* that is, the Consciousness assumes the form of 4th state of Consciousness, and when it degrades to *World 12* cosmos level it assumes the form of 3rd state of Consciousness, and when it still degrades to *World 24* cosmos level it assumes the form of relaxed, controlled & directed Attention, and so on.

Therefore, under the *States of Consciousness* heading, at *World 6* level it has been placed as 4th state of Consciousness; at the next below level of *World 12,* it has been placed as 3rd state of Consciousness; at the next below level of *World 24* it has been placed as relaxed, controlled & directed attention, and so on.

Likewise all other significant esoteric ideas have been presented. And the material aspect also (on the Creation and then on its devolution at various cosmos levels) has been presented in the same way.

So, all the Diagrams put together give overall picture of the ***organic whole*** of both, the Spiritual (psychological) aspect and the Material aspect of Man and the Universe.

About the enneagrams

The Enneagram is a pictorial way of showing simultaneous operation of the law of three, that is, how the three forces combine and produce six processes; and the operation of law of seven, that is, sequential occurrence of six processes in time.

The quality of resultant six processes and of their further degradation depends on the quality of the three forces. For example, when purest Satva (4th state of consciousness), purest Rajasa (conscious wish) and purest Tamasa (self-remembrance and unity) combine as three forces, it produces the six activities of evolved man, as against the activities of ordinary man where the three forces of much lower quality combine.

The Law of Seven is a universal law applicable everywhere, the crux of which is that, when any thing proceeds in time, it proceeds in Octave, that is, in a sequence of seven notes of the same octave and one note of the next octave, with 2 intervals in between. At these two intervals the progression of the course of events stops or changes direction, if those intervals are not bridged with extra and new kinds of efforts. Octave proceeds in this order: Do Re Mi – Fa Sol La Si – Do. The 1st interval occurs between note Mi and Fa, and 2nd interval occurs at the end, after note Si, that is, before the starting of next new octave.

Every phenomenon, material or psychological, proceeds as per the Law of Seven. And so, in every phenomena there are 2 intervals where the progression of the course of events stops or changes direction, if the intervals are not bridged with extra and new kinds of efforts.

Like any other phenomenon, the three forces, Temperature (1st force), Activation Energy barrier (2nd force) and Catalyst (3rd force) produce basic six types of Chemical Reactions namely, (1) Single Displacement - 2-3-1, (2) Acid-base neutralization - 3-1-2, (3) Decomposition - 1-2-3, (4) Combustion - 1-3-2, (5) Synthesis - 3-2-1 and (6) Double Displacement - 2-1-3.

(To understand why the Acid-base Neutralization Reaction is "3-1-2" process, and to understand the basic nature of various processes in general, see explanations given against various *Chakras* in the Diagram of Location of Process Points in human organism.)

The use of terms

In this book certain terms carry special meaning as against their usual day-to-day meaning. For example, *Identification,* which ordinarily means, "Process of establishing the identity of someone or something", but, here this term means, "The process of loosing oneself; becoming one with particular thought, emotion, impulse, outside object, situation etc.; and in that moment not having capacity to keep the sense of Self separate and detached from that thought, emotion, impulse, outside object, situation, etc."

For instance, when we are watching live World Cup Final Match of our favorite game, at critical moments of such match how much *identified* we become! Or when two people are arguing heatedly over something or trying to prove something vehemently, how much *identified* they become with their words, opinions or arguments! Identification is one of our most terrible & difficult foes because it penetrates everywhere, in our every action. When one is too much identified, one can not act sensibly and can not see things as they are. Further, the identification has degrees, sometimes one is more *identified*, sometimes less.

Many other terms have been used in the same way, like: *Worlds*, the Ray of Creation, Degree of Immortality, False Personality, True Personality, The Essence, Consciousness, Presence, Higher Centers, four Lower Centers, Density of Maya, six Processes, Impressions, Hydrogen, Body-types, Chief Features, Center of Gravity, Essence Activity, Body-type Activity, *Formatory* thinking, Influence A, Influence B, Influence C, Scale & Relativity, Level of Being, *Satva-Rajasa-Tamasa* (three forces), Many "I"s, Work "I"s, etc.

Following Explanatory Notes attempt to explain the special meaning which such terms carry, apart from explaining other important esoteric concepts.

The diagrams for the most part precede the text that explains them.

About the 4th Way

The 4th Way is a way of spiritual/psychological evolution by knowing and understanding within oneself the Intellect, Emotion & Physical impulse; rightly balancing their workings; learning to apply them all simultaneously in unified manner in day-to-day activities with intentional and enhanced awareness (attention/consciousness); and thereby eventually attaining spiritual purity and higher states of consciousness.

In 20th Century G. I. Gurdjieff and P. D. Ouspensky expounded the 4th Way in their teachings and writings, which was further elaborated and refined in the writings of Rodney Collin.

Section I: Cosmology

The Ray of Creation (*Utpatisarga*)					
Sr. No.	**World**	**4th Way Description**	**Eastern/ Hindu Description**	**Corresponding Energy/ Matter**	**Life (In Human Years)**
			**ParamBrahm* THE ALMIGHTY		
1	World1	The Absolute	**AksharBrahm (Brahmrup)*	*Chidakash*	Imperishable
2	World3	All Worlds (All Galaxies)	*PrakritiPurush -MulPurush* ***(Kaivalya)***	Quantum (elementary particle)	World 6 * 36000
3	World6	All Suns (Our Galaxy) (Milky Way)	*PradhanPurush* *(***Aishwarya***)*	Nuclear	311040 * 36000 Billion (Day of *Mulpurush*) (***Atyantik Pralaya***)
4	World12	Our Sun (Solar System)	*ViratPurush -Mahatatva* (**Divinity**)	Atomic	311040 Billion (Day of *Pradhan*) (***Prakrut Pralaya***)
5	World24	All Planets (Planetary Sphere)	*Manu, Indra Ashmita* - Innocence (**Essence**)	Molecular	864 Crore (Day of *ViratBrahmaa*) (***Nimitt Pralaya***)
6	World48	Organic Life on Earth (the Nature)	**Jiva* – Good Householder (**True Personality**)	Cellular	24 Lac (*Pal* of *ViratBrahmaa*) (***Nitya Pralaya***)
7	World96	Moon	False Ego - Ordinary Man (Lower self) (**False Personality**)	Solid Matter	

Note: *ViratBrahmaa* is living beings on *World 6* level, like man is living being on *World 48* level. 1 pal (few moments) of *ViratBrahmaa* = 24 lac human years (*Nitya Pralay*), 24 hours of *ViratBrahmaa* = 864 crore human years (*Nimitt Pralay*) and life of 100 years of *ViratBrahmaa* = 311040 billion human years (*Prakrut Pralay*). The Ray of Creation proceeds downward from top to bottom.

The Ray of Creation

The Ray of Creation issues from the Absolute, the *AksharBrahm* (Existence, Non-existence, Manifest and Un-manifest all taken together); from that comes infinite number of *All Words* (all known and unknown multitude of Galaxies all taken together); from that comes Milky Way (our Galaxy of all Suns taken together); from that comes our Sun; from that comes all Planets taken together, our Earth, Organic Life on Earth (the Nature), and the Moon. (On the basis of this principle, probably there are 12 types of Planets (Planetary objects), 6 categories of Solar Systems, and 3 categories of Galaxies). Please refer to the Diagram of The Ray of Creation (*Utpatisarga*).

We have taken the Ray of Creation from the view point of our Earth. There may be infinite number of such Rays of Creation. The Ray of Creation is termed as *Utpatisarga* in *Vedanta* Hindu Texts. In the Bhagwad Geeta – XV (1 and 2), the Ray of Creation is termed as *Urdhvamulam AdhahShakham Ashwastham* (that is, such banyan tree which has the root at the top, and branches spreading downwards), and the verse XV (1) of the Bhagwad Geeta says that the person who rightly understands the Ray of Creation is the knower of the essence of *Vedas*.

Human body is constituted by innumerous independently living body Cells. They all live comfortably like we live, and the physical mass of all of them together form a living human body, but they can not directly see Man as we see ourselves (a cross-section of human body is visible world for cells). In the same way we all human beings and entire organic life constitute a living being, the Earth. What we can see of Earth is only a cross-section of its living body. In the same way the multitude of all known and unknown planets constitute a living being, the Sun. What we see as Sun is but a cross-section of a cross-section of its living body. Likewise is the Milky way and *All Worlds*.

These all progressive GREATER BEINGS are various *Ishwara* grades, e.g. *ViratBrahmaa* is a being (*Ishwara*) living on the level of *World* 6 (i.e. Galaxy Level). As one evolves, one progressively attains the level of consciousness, bliss and relative immortality (not size) of these Greater Beings.

Man has three bodies gross, subtle and causal. In ordinary man one's *Jiva* (life principle) is fused and crystallised in cellular matter, the subtle body is reflected only as mind activity, and the causal body is reflected only as Essence.

As one evolves to the level of Man No. 5, the potential of one's subtle body develops fully and one's *Jiva* fuses and crystallises into molecular energy (chiefly by transmutation of suffering, negative emotions and sex energy), and it becomes Astral Body; and as one evolves to the level of Man No. 6, the potential of causal body starts developing and one's *Jiva* fuses and crystallises into electron energy (chiefly by dying to one's Lower self and by being re-born); and at the level of Man No. 7, one's causal body becomes fully developed *Vigyan* Body.

Atman (the Spirit) is beyond these three bodies. *AksharBrahm* is beyond *Atman* (the Spirit), and *ParamBrahm* is beyond *AksharBrahm* (the Bhagwad Geeta – XV -18). In its true and full sense, only *ParamBrahm* is THE ALMIGHTY.

As par Hindu Texts, as like men has gross, subtle and causal bodies, *Ishwaras* (GREATER BEINGS) have *Virata* (enormously Huge corresponding physical body), *Sutratma* (that which binds the whole together, corresponding subtle body) and *Avyakrut* (corresponding causal body). Like man, *Ishwara* also needs to evolve to reach to the next respective higher level of being in their own way. Below the level of the Absolute (*AksharBrahm*), everything is relative and has degrees.

Theoretically, for spiritual evolution the faith and belief in THE ALMIGHTY, is not compulsory. But practically, for a theist evolution become easier, if his faith and belief is with understanding and is not merely escapism. An atheist can evolve upto the level of Man No. 8, if he understands the Grand Scheme of Creation of Cosmoses, and makes right efforts. But, without ultimate *fana* in *Brahmrup* devotion towards *ParamBrahm*, THE ALMIGHTY, it is not possible for anyone to attain the level of Man No. 9. However, one's understanding of THE ALMIGHTY can be relative only, according to one's level of being, and so is one's faith and belief in HIM.

Spiritual-Psychological (Chaitanya) aspect of the Creation

As the Creation progresses, on Spiritual-Psychological (*Chaitanya*) side, *Purusha* (Spirit), *Prakriti* (*Maya*) and *Kal* (Time) becomes denser and denser and operates as the three Forces, *Kal* being the 2nd Force (Passive Force) *Prakriti* being the 1st Force (Active Force) and *Purusha* being the 3rd Force (Neutralising Force). *Kal* (Time) is a kind of mysterious faculty of THE ALMIGHTY.

At each stage of Creation the *Maya* veils the Spirit (Sense of Self - *Atmbhav*) more and more, and hence, the Spirit (*Atman*) assumes the form of state of consciousness; the *Karma* (being result of *Prakriti* acting) becomes less and less pure (Bliss being the purest *Karma*, then comes Love, Hope and Will and so on); and the grade of *Kal* (Time) becomes lower and lower i.e. the depth and expand of self-remembrance becomes less and less and the life span (immortality) becomes shorter and shorter. Please refer to the Diagram of The Ladder of Evolution.

Active force means the force which initiates action; Passive force means the force which resists or opposes the action, or which is the material on which the action is being performed; and Neutralising force means a force which acts as formative and balancing element in the process, or is the medium or atmosphere in which the action is being performed. No action or event can take place without the combining of the three forces.

In man's psychological side three forces reflect as *Triguna* (*Satva, Rajasa* and *Tamasa*). *Satva* is reflected as consciousness (attention in ordinary man), *Rajasa* is reflected as will (desire, craving and restlessness in ordinary man), and *Tamasa* is reflected as self-remembrance and unity (lethargy, delusion and ignorance in ordinary man).

In this book we have used the term Carbon (C) for Active Force, Oxygen (O) for Passive Force, Nitrogen (N) for Neutralising Force and Hydrogen (H) for the Unification of the three forces. (For example, C = Heat, O = Flour, N = Water and H = Bread. For more details please refer to the Explanatory Note on Hydrogen).

By nature *Rajasa* is C, Active; *Tamas* is O, Passive and *Satva* is N, Neutralising; but any Force can occupy any other's place. Six Processes arise as a result of the Three Forces combining in various ways. (2-3-1= Healing, 3-1-2 = Crime/Disease, 1-2-3 = Growth, 1-3-2 = Destruction, 3-2-1 = Regeneration and 2-1-3 = Refinement). The nature of various processes has been dealt with in detail by Rodney Collin in his book, *The Theory of Celestial Influence* (pages from 172 to 203), published by SHAMBHALA, Boulder and London, 1984.

If one works on oneself (does *Sadhna*) under right guidance and grace for a sufficiently long time, possibility of reversal of this process arises and the spiritual evolution becomes possible for him.

Material (Jad) aspect of the Creation

The Creation is a descending octave, a growth process; on Material side, due to the Energy Binding Mechanism, the matter aspect becomes denser and grosser, and the energy aspect becomes less and less manifest, as it devolves on each next stage of Creation.

In the Material Devolution process the Temperature acts as Active force (1st force), Energy Binding Mechanism acts as Passive force (2nd force) and the Time/Space (a kind of mysterious faculty of THE ALMIGHTY) acts as the Neutralising force (3rd force); effecting reduction in the Temperature by passage of time, and thereby creating various grades of matter and various Worlds of progressive levels.

However, at World 1 (The Absolute) level, there is no Time/Space duality, so, everything is Chidakash (alive nothingness).

As the element of time enters, the sum total of passage of Time becomes the Space. The passage of Time, i.e. the Space, brings the Temperature down to the point where the Matter comes into being in Quantum (basic elementary particle, by whatever name we may call it) state, which contains all the possibilities. This process amounts to, and results into, the creation of numerous World 3 (all Galaxies taken together).

With further passage of Time the Temperature comes further down, and the formation of free protons, antiproton, neutrons, antineutrons, electrons and positron takes place; and also the Energy Binding Mechanism comes into existence, by which tremendous amount of energy from the system gets *locked* in the mechanism of binding protons and neutrons together into Nucleus, overcoming mutual repulsion of protons (that is, Nuclear Binding Energy), which reflects as, what is called in Nuclear Physics, the *mass defect*. This process amounts to, and results into, the creation of numerous *World 6* (Galaxy, like the Milky Way), having matter in nuclear state, and having its own time (2nd grade Time, i.e. sub-time within the Time of *World 3*). Due to the locking *up* of energy in Nuclear Binding Mechanism, the nuclear matter becomes grosser than the quantum (elementary basic particles).

At *World 6* (Galaxy) level the nucleus of any element can at any time become the nucleus of any other element, e. g. nucleus of hydrogen can at any time become nucleus of oxygen, or nucleus of iron can any time become nucleus of gold and so on.

With the passage of *World 6*'s Time the Temperature comes down further, and further considerable amount of energy from the system gets *locked* in the mechanism of binding electrons around nucleus (that is, Electron Binding Energy) to form atoms of various elements. This process amounts to, and results into, the creation of numerous *World 12* (the Sun), having matter in atomic state, and having its own time (3rd grade Time, i.e. sub-time within the Time of *World*

6). Due to further *locking up* of energy in Electron Binding Mechanism, the atomic matter becomes grosser than the nuclear matter.

With the passage of World 12's Time the Temperature comes still further down, and certain further amount of energy gets locked in the mechanism of binding atoms together by Chemical Bonds caused by electromagnetic force forming molecules of various chemical compounds. This process amounts to, and results into, the creation of numerous World 24 (planetary sphere), having matter in molecular state, and having its own time (4th grade Time, i.e. sub-time within the Time of World 12). Due to further locking up of energy in Chemical Bonding Mechanism, the molecular matter becomes grosser than the atomic matter.

At *World 24* (Planetary sphere) level the molecule of one chemical compound can at any time become the molecule of other chemical compound containing atoms of same elements but with different structure.

With the passage of *World 24*'s time, by the fusion of molecular matter with *Jiva* (life principle), the cellular (*JadChidatmak*, that is, fusion of life and matter together) matter comes into being. This process amounts to, and results into, the creation of *World 48* (Organic life on Earth, the Nature, of which man is a part), having matter in cellular state, and having its own time (5th grade Time, i.e. sub-time within the Time of *World 24*). And also molecules solidify into Solid Matters. The moon is *World 96*, acting as balance weight for the Organic life and the Earth.

So, our time, the human time is 5th grade time, that is, a time within time of *World 24* (4th grade time), which itself is within time of *World 12* (3rd grade time), which itself is within time of *World 6* (2nd grade time), which itself is within time of *World 3* (1st grade time). Comparison between lives of various *Worlds* in terms of human years has been shown in the Diagram of the Ray of Creation (*Utpatisarga*). And the dimensional aspect of time at various *Worlds* has been shown in the Diagram of Density of Maya (the Web of Laws) and Time/ Space.

As the matter degrades more and more, its properties become more and more fixed, and so, its possibilities become more and more limited.

As the energy and the matter (mass) are two aspects of the same thing, the grossest matter contain in itself enormous un-manifested energy (that is, energy *locked* in Binding Mechanism) as explained by Mr. Albert Einstein in E=mc2. In the same way, each living being contains deep down enormous un-manifest (un-actualised) *Chaitanya* (Consciousness) energy.

When the matter is brought back to the higher level by special efforts, energy of the one level below is released e.g. when atoms are split, the atomic energy is released; and in the process of fusion/fission of two or more atomic nucleus, the nuclear energy is released. For example, invention and explosion of hydrogen bomb is the creation of *World 12* material energy on the Earth, in other words, creation of hydrogen bomb amounts to creation of *miniature sun* on the Earth.

If and when the science will develop to the point where it can bring back the matter to the *controlled and manipulable fluid nuclear* state, it would be able to convert iron into gold, in other words, this would be like creation of *miniature galaxy* on the Earth.

Combined reading of the Law of Three, Scale and Relativity, Space-Time duality and the concept of *AksharBrahm,* along with the material we already have in the field of physics and chemistry, unfolds the above overall picture of the Material aspect of the Creation, and at the same time it synthesizes, connects and places various information at their exact relative place in the picture of the whole.

Correspondence between Material and Psychological Phenomena

The psychological phenomena of learning and practically applying the process of bringing *ChittVriti* (essence of attention) back to oneself, that is, dividing attention, or keeping sense of self separate from thought, emotion, impulse, outside object, situation, etc. is equivalent to the material phenomena of invention of Electricity.

Likewise, the psychological phenomenon of learning and practically applying the process of transmutation of suffering and negative emotions into positive emotions (positive emotions means such emotions which can not becomes negative again) of conscious love, conscious wish, conscious hope, etc. is equivalent to the material phenomena of invention and peaceful use of nuclear energy in such a way that it doesn't result into any hazard to the environment.

The difference of presently available advanced material facilities attributable to the invention of Electricity, Nuclear energy and other consequential inventions, from the poor material facilities that were available 200 years ago; is exactly the corresponding difference of inner psychological richness of Man No. 5

attributable to self-remembering and transmutation, from the inner psychological poverty of Man No. 1, 2 and 3.

To understand the difference between inner life of Man No.7 and Man No. 1, 2, or 3 through material analogy, let us visualise (as compared to the poor material facilities that were available 200 years ago) the kind of richness, ease and advancement of material facilities that would be available in our world, if the science as a whole is developed to the point that the solar energy can be abundantly and freely converted into Electricity with no or minimal cost; and if the iron or any other matter can be easily converted into gold or any other matter; and if any material substance like platinum, diamond, etc. can be *manufactured* easily and freely (it is equivalent to the creation of *miniature galaxy* on the Earth); and also there is completely fair and just civil life without any criminal activity, and without any environmental pollution! Such vast is the difference between inner life of Man No. 7 and Man No. 1, 2 or 3!

On material side we have already witnessed the adverse consequences on the mankind and environment of the misuse of nuclear energy and other inventions. But, fortunately, on psychological side there is no possibility of such misuse of spiritual powers, as the evolution itself is the result of equivalent purity of one's being. Moreover, the very nature of spiritual evolution being inner and personal, its results are also inner and personal to oneself, unlike Material advancement.

From another view point, the process of chemical reaction in which required temperature, catalysts, etc. are applied to bring back the particular chemical compound (*World 48* material) to higher level (that is, free molecular level, *World 24* level) where it can be converted into desired chemical compound by electron exchange mechanism; is quite analogous to the psychological process of applying consciousness (by effort of self-remembering, divided attention, presence, etc.) for melting particular fixed opinion (that is, psychological energy of *World 48*) and bringing it back to fine emotion (that is, psychological energy of *World 24*), and thereby converting that fixed opinion into open mindedness.

In the same way, on higher order, the process of fusion/fission of nucleus, in which, by applying special efforts of breaking the Nuclear Binding Energy barrier, the matter is brought back to nuclear level (*World 6* level) where the fusion of two light nucleus into one heavier nucleus, or the fission of one heavier nucleus into two or more lighter nucleus become possible, releasing in the system tremendously powerful nuclear energy (so far which was lying *locked* in Nuclear Binding Mechanism); is quite analogous to the psychological process of applying the special advanced efforts of transmutation of negative emotions into positive emotions by bringing that psychological matter (negative emotions) back to *World 6* energy level (by breaking the barrier of Lower-self Sustaining Mechanism) where the transmutation of negative emotions into positive emotions (that is, psychological energy of *World 12*) become possible, releasing within one's organism the profound energy of sustained 3rd state of consciousness (so far which was lying *locked* in Lower-self Sustaining Mechanism).

Fixation of particular opinion is analogous to the Chemical Bonding Mechanism, fixation of fine emotions within the limitations of one's Body-type is analogous to the Electron Binding Mechanism, and the *Lower self Sustaining Mechanism* is analogous to the Nuclear Binding Mechanism, and so, breaking them needs progressively much higher order of efforts. The Nuclear Binding Energy is on the order of a million times greater than the Electron Binding Energy.

And also, the psychological equivalent of physically turning iron into gold is the cessation of negative emotions of *Kama* (lust), *Krodha* (wrath), *Lobha* (greed), *Moha* (illusion), *Mad* (vanity), *Asha* (wrongly placed wish), *Trishna* (passions), *Irshya* (envy), *Ahankar* (false ego) etc. attributable to the conscious death of one's Lower self.

Density of Maya (the Web of laws) & Time/Space					
Sr. No	**World**	**No of Orders of Law (Density of *Maya) (Reflected in Universe)**	**No of Orders of Law (Density of *Maya) (Reflected in Man)**	**Dimensions of Time/ Space (for Man)**	**Division of our Time into**
1	World1	1 (Indivisible Whole)	1 (No Law/ No Maya)	Beyond Time & Space	
2	World3	3 (Three Forces)	3 (Spirit-Space-Time)	Infinite Eternities (6th Dimension)	3 Seasons
3	World6	3+3=6 (6 Basic Processes)	3+3=6 (6/*Shat Chakras*) (Ability to Do - *Siddhis*)	Eternity (5th Dimension)	6 *Ritus* (sub-seasons)
4	World12	3+6+3=12 (12 Body-Types)	3+6+3=12 (One's Body-type Activity) (One's Will)	Passage of Time (4th Dimension)	12 Months
5	World24	3+6+12+3=24 (Pendulum of 12 Essence Activities & 12 Chief Features) (fine Emotions) (Fine works of Arts)	3+6+12+3=24 (Pendulum between one's Essence Activity & Chief Feature) (One's Emotions & Sensitivity)	Depth - visible Space (3rd Dimension)	24 Moon Waxing-Waning
6	World48	3+6+12+24+3=48 (48 Centre of Gravities - mental outlooks) (Day to day Civilized life)	3+6+12+24+3= 48 (One's Practical thinking & right Attitude)	Width - Plane/ Surface (2nd Dimension)	48 Day/ Nights of Moon Waxing-Waning
7	World96	3+6+12+24+48+3=96 (96 basic Types of Passions/ Impulses) (Criminal & Spoilage Activities)	3+6+12+24+48 +3=96 (One's Negative Emotions/ Passions) (*Formatory* thinking) (One's Lower self)	Length - Line (1st Dimension)	Spoilage of Seasons by Atmospheric Pollution

Density of Maya (the Web of Laws) and the naming of various Worlds

Naming of various Worlds has been done on the basis of number of laws prevailing in that particular World (in other words, on the basis of density of Maya prevailing in that particular World). More the orders of laws are prevailing, the density of Maya is more, the matter is denser, and the level of being is lower. The reflection of density of Maya in Man and Universe at various levels of being is shown in the Diagram of Density of Maya (the Web of Laws) and Space/Time.

The Absolute (*AksharBrahm*) is named as ***World 1***, as there is only 1 law, that is, everything is one, in other words *Maya* does not exist there, and everything is *living*.

The next *World* is named as ***World 3***, (there are infinite number of such ***World 3***s) where only 3 laws are prevailing, *Maya* is at its purest form (in the form of *GunaSamya Prakriti*, that is, *Satva-Rajasa-Tamasa* (three forces) are at equated and integrated state), on material side the matter is in its purest form i.e. in the quantum (elementary basic particles, by whatever name we may call it) state.

The next *World* is named as ***World 6*** (within one ***World 3***, there are infinite no. of such ***World 6***s), where 3 laws of next order enter and total no of laws become 6, (that is, 3 laws of ***World3*** plus ***World 6***'s own 3 laws), *Maya* starts becoming denser, and assumes the form of purest but separated *Satva* (N), *Rajasa* (C) and *Tamasa* (O) (that is, 4th state of Consciousness (N), Conscious wish (C) and Miraculous ability to do - *Siddhis* (O); on material side the matter start getting dense and devolves to the nucleus state.

The next *World* is named as ***World 12*** (within one ***World 6***, there are infinite no. of such ***World 12***s), where 3 laws of next order enter and total no of laws become 12 (that is, 3 laws of ***World3*** plus 6 laws of ***World 6*** plus ***World 12***'s own 3 laws), *Maya* becomes more dense and *Satva* (N), *Rajasa* (C) and *Tamasa* (O) degrades and assumes the form of the 3rd state of consciousness (N), will (C) and the unity (O); on material side the matter becomes more dense and devolves to the atomic state.

The next *World* is named as ***World 24*** (within one ***World 12***, there are infinite no. of such ***World 24***s), where 3 laws of next order enter and total no of laws become 24 (that is, 3 laws of ***World3*** plus 6 laws of ***World 6*** plus 12 laws of ***World 12*** plus ***World 24***'s own 3 laws), *Maya* becomes more dense and *Satva* (N), *Rajasa* (C) and *Tamasa* (O) degrades further and assumes the form of faith and self-belief (N), permanent tendency (C) and care and sensitivity (O); on material side the matter becomes more dense and devolves to the molecular state.

The next *World* is named as ***World 48***, where 3 laws of next order enter and total no of laws become 48 (that is, 3 laws of ***World3*** plus 6 laws of ***World 6*** plus 12 laws of ***World 12*** plus 24 laws of ***World 24*** plus ***World 48***'s own 3 laws), *Maya* becomes still more dense and *Satva* (N), *Rajasa* (C) and *Tamasa* (O) degrades still further and assumes the form of controlled and directed attention (N), Magnetic Centre (*Khap-Mumukshuta*) and desire (C) and mechanical-ness of Chief Feature (O); on material side the cellular matter comes into being by fusion of molecular matter and the *Jiva* (life principle).

The next *World* is named as ***World 96***, where 3 laws of next order enter and total no of laws become 96 (that is, 3 laws of ***World3*** plus 6 laws of ***World 6*** plus 12 laws of ***World 12*** plus 24 laws of ***World 24*** plus 48 laws of ***World 48*** plus ***World 96***'s own 3 laws), *Maya* becomes densest and *Satva* (N), *Rajasa* (C) and *Tamasa* (O) degrades to the lowest level and assumes the form of fascinated or very little attention (N), craving (C) and utter mechanical-ness of Chief Feature (O); on material side the matter becomes still more dense and solidifies into Solid state.

Dimensions of Space and Time

Basically space and time are two aspects of the same thing. Man has three dimensional view: man can see three dimensions of a thing in space, i.e. at a time. The relation between two progressive dimensions is that of zero to infinity. The 1st dimension is a line, infinity of a point; the 2nd dimension is a surface, infinity of a line; the 3rd dimension is a solid, infinity of a surface; the 4th dimension is infinity of a solid. For us movement of a solid occurs in time, we can see 4th dimension occurring in time, for us the passage of our time is the 4th dimension. The 5th dimension is a solid's infinity's infinity, for us the 5th dimension is our eternity. The 6th dimension is *All*, where all possibilities are realised and fulfilled (including creation and fulfillment of new ones); for us the 6th dimension is our infinite eternities. Please refer to the Diagram of Density of Maya (the web of laws) and Time/Space.

Physically also, each Cosmos has one dimension higher than immediate lower Cosmos, for example, if we take a man as point then its infinity (that is, entire mankind and organic life taken together) is line, the next higher dimension. Man has one dimension higher than cell, the Nature has one dimension higher than man, and the Earth has one dimension higher than the Nature and two dimensions higher than man, and so on.

A cross-section of immediate higher Cosmos, at right angle to that lower Cosmos's position, represents the *present visible world* for that lower Cosmos e.g. what we see in this moment as our *present visible world* is a cross-section of the Nature at right angle to us; in the same way, a cross-section of human body at right angles to cells represents the present visible world for cells. Other cross-sections higher up is the future (coming into being moment to moment), and cross-sections lower down is the past (what has happened and gone).

To understand the relation between cross-section and the larger body, let us take an example of series of photos constituting the movie. In movie 24 photos (frames) passes in front of our eyes in a series per second and give us the impression of picture in motion. Each individual still photo of the movie is a cross-section of the *larger cosmos of that movie*. In other words, the cosmos of that movie is made up of numerous photos (cross-sections) taken in a series at a rate of 24 photos (frames) per second. If one has not viewed that particular movie (cosmos), then one can not recognise that this particular photo (a cross-section) is part of that movie (cosmos), and can not understand the exact place which it occupies in that movie (cosmos). In our example, viewing individual still photo (frame) is one dimension, and viewing those all photos (frames) in movie form is its next higher dimension. This example shows the relation between two dimensions.

Man's 4th dimension (man's passage of time) is 3rd dimension for the Nature i.e. the Nature can see whole life of man as solid, in space. The Nature's 4th dimension (the Nature's passage of time and man's eternity) is 3rd dimension for the Earth i.e. the Earth can see whole life of the Nature and eternity of man as solid, in space. The Earth's 4th dimension (the Earth's passage of time, the Nature's eternity and man's All possibilities) is 3rd dimension for the Sun i.e. the Sun can see whole life of the Earth, eternity of the Nature and man's all possibilities as solid, in space, and so on.

For more details on this subject one may refer to Rodney Collin's book, *The Theory of Celestial Influence* (pages from 19 to 34), published by SHAMBHALA, Boulder and London, 1984.

Quality of various orders of Space

There exist series of qualities of space, one within another. The space of *World 1* is the purest and most illumined, and is *living nothingness*. But in the space of *World 3* denser matter of its own order enters and thus the quality of its space become little less pure and less illumined. In the space of world 6, still denser matter of its own order enters. In the space of world 12, still denser matter of its own order enters. In the space of world 24, still denser matter of its own order enters. In the space of world 48, still denser matter (air and atmosphere of the earth) of its own order enters. In the space of world 96, still denser matter of its own order enters.

All these matters are invisible to our naked eye. This way, in the space of every order new matter of its own enters and makes the space denser and denser, and less and less illumined. And thus the series of qualities of space is created.

So when we use word ***space*** it implies and includes in it the basic matters as stated above. For example, when we say the space of world 12, we mean the space permeated by the basic and invisible matters of *World 1, World 3, World 6 and World 12*. Thus the matters of all the above worlds permeate the space we see now in front of us. So, creating vacuum (which has degrees) means removing these invisible matters from the space.

Inter-relation between various Cosmoses

Man is Sun for Electron

Man is Earth for Molecule

Man is Nature for Cell

Man is Cell for the Nature

Man is Molecule for the Earth

Man is Electron for the Sun

Concept of Life and Matter (*Chaitanya* and *Jad*)

Like all other aspects, the concept of living and non-living is also relative. On the Earth we take Organic Life as living and buildings and other such material things as non-living, and this is very much true from human point of view, but from the point of view of the Earth, all material things and entire Organic Life is part of its whole body, and so for the Earth everything that we see here on the Earth is alive. For the Earth other Planets, Asteroids and space objects that we consider moving, may be living, and stationary molecular matter may be non-living material; which in tern is also a part of the body of the Sun, and so for the Sun everything existing within our Solar System is living, and so on. For the Absolute (*Akshar Brahm*), everything is living.

Likewise for us our entire body is a living organism, but for constituent cells all moving cells like blood cells, lymph cells etc. may be living ones and stationary cells like that of muscles and other organs may be non-living ones, like we here have mountains, natural lakes etc.! Here, on the Earth (i.e. within the Earth's body) there are criminals, and criminal and spoilage activity, in the same way within the human body there are diseases and disease affected cells.

Place and luck of Human Being in the entire Scheme of Cosmoses

Human being is at mid-point in the whole scheme of Cosmoses. Below human being in the scheme of Cosmoses is cell, molecule, electron, nucleus and quantum (elementary basic particle); and above him is the Nature, the Earth and other planets, the Sun, the Milky Way (Galaxy) and All Worlds (All Galaxies). It is said time and again in various esoteric writings that man is made in the Image of the GOD. Each and every material and energy that exists in the Universe also exist in a human being in different proportions as a matter of his basic constitution (for usual proportion in ordinary man, see in the Diagram of Quality of Impressions and their effects).

To be born as a human being is a great luck, it is said that even gods wish to be born as human beings because human being has potential to evolve fully (only if one could realise and make right and sufficient efforts to materialise it). But generally we take our being born as human for granted, for example, we take the electricity for granted; we switch on/off a tube-light, fan, air-conditioner or any other electric apparatus, but never take a pause to realise that behind such a simple act of switching on/off, what tremendous research work and taming of higher material energy has gone into!

If we could re-alive in ourselves this feeling of awe, whenever and wherever possible, by just trying to pause and realise what have really gone behind the things; it will give our being certain humility, depth and ability to grasp more. We all human beings are much more luckier than we generally think.

The process of birth of human embryo, fertilisation of human ovum by a sperm, takes place by way of meeting of three forces; Sperm is Active Force (1st force), ovum is Passive Force (2nd force) and presence of sex energy (*World 12* energy), or a artificially created condition in case of artificial fertilisation, is Neutralising Force (3rd force); In this process, by the fusion of two cellular level *Jivas*, the entry and re-birth of human level *Jiva* takes place, at cellular energy level.

In the same way, the process of birth of Astral body inside human being by transmutation of suffering and negative emotions takes place by way of meeting of three forces; Mi 12 (of impression octave) contained in intense suffering or negative emotion is Active Force, Sol 12 (of air octave) is Passive Force and the presence of compassionate *World 12* energy produced by effort of self-remembrance and separation from suffering or negative emotions is Neutralising Force.

Likewise, the process of birth of Astral body by *Brahmcharya* (celibacy - transmutation of sex energy) takes place by way of meeting of three forces; Si 12 (of food octave) contained in intense sex drive is Active Force, Sol 12 (of air octave) is Passive Force and the presence of devotional *World 12* energy produced by effort of god-remembrance and separation from sex energy is Neutralising Force.

In both these processes, human *Jiva* fuses and crystallises into Molecular energy level, as here three molecules fuses together and give birth to a new being, the astral body. Once the birth of astral body has taken place, it grows further by the same transmutation efforts.

For exact details as to what is meant by Si 12 (of food octave), Sol 12 (of air octave) and Mi 12 (of impression octave), one may refer to Chapter 9 (page 167 to 198) of the book, *In the Search of the Miraculous* written by P. D. Ouspensky, published by Harcourt, Inc. (San Diego, New York and London).

The Alchemy of body-chemistry

In ordinary man, chemical compounds that are responsible for various negative emotions are in a fixed chemical state, and its nature always remains the same, so when the expression of negative emotion is not allowed in one way, it slips and finds its expression in another way. But, when one transforms negative emotions the alchemical changes takes place in one's body-chemistry.

When one transforms suffering or negative emotions into positive emotions, that time one is bringing that chemical compound in a *free atomic state;* by *holding* that volatile energy of suffering or negative emotion within, and applying the process of *chemical reaction* through the energy of higher consciousness; so the very nature of that chemical compound converts into something of very high order, and that *alchemical material* thus converted becomes available in the form of increased consciousness, love and Presence. Such free molecular alchemical material constitutes the Astral body.

The Process of Multiplicity from the Unity				
Sr. No	**World**		**In Cosmos**	**In Man (Microcosmos)**
		0	*ParamBrahm*	*ParamAtman*
1	World1	**1**	*Brahm* (basic Unity)	*Atman* (Spirit)
2	World3	**2**	*Chaitanya* & *Jad*; Life & Matter (basic Duality)	*Atman* (Spirit) & Body
3	World6	**3**	Forces (Active, Passive & Neutralising) - the Law of Three	*Kaph, Pitt* & *Vatt* – *Tamasa, Satva* & *Rajasa* - Love, Wish & Hope - Consciousness, Will & Unity
4	World12	**4**	States of Matter (3 carrying forces + their Unification)	Kaph, Pitt, Vatt + Unified Mind (ONC + H) (Wordless breaths)
5	World24	**5**	The Elements (Space, Air, Fire, Water & Earth)	Sex, Intellectual, Moving, Emotional & Instinctive Center (Un-unified Mind); 5 Senses; 5 *Karmendriya*
		6	6 Processes; 6 *Ritus*; 6 Tastes; 6 types of Chemical Reactions; 6 Karmas (Moon, Mercury, Venus, Mars, Jupiter & Saturn); Utterance of Work "I"s in a Sequence	*Agya Chakra, Vishuddhi Chakra, Anahat Chakra, Manipur Chakra, Swadhisthan Chakra* & *Muladhar Chakra* (reflected in Essence Activities & Features)
6	World48	**7**	(6 Processes + Passage of Time = The Law of Seven)	Man in Time (Process of wishing & living)
		8	Completed Octave (Do Re Mi Fa Sol La Si Do)	Actions moving in intended direction
7	World96	**9**	Octave with 2 Intervals (Do Re Mi - Fa Sol La Si -) Sun; Moon; Mars; *Rahu* - North Node; Jupiter; Saturn; Mercury; Venus; *Ketu* - South Node (Eastern *Nakchhatra*-Constellation Sequence)	Actions deviating from intended direction (Mechanical & Accidental Actions)

Formatory Thinking

Formatory thinking means mechanical and narrow logical thinking without attention. It has certain peculiarities, like comparing only two things as if in that particular line only two things exist; thinking in extremes, for instance, either knowing everything or knowing nothing; and immediately looking for opposites etc. We can find many examples of formatory thinking. For example, if some one says, you must do this or must do that, he says "But you yourself said that we can not do!" If someone suggests that you should try to be more conscious than you are, he says, "But we have no consciousness!"

Higher esoteric ideas can not be understood by using *formatory* thinking; it needs at least much better focused intentional thinking with controlled and directed attention.

Kinds of Influence

As explained by P. D. Ouspensky in his book *In the Search of the Miraculous,* published by Harcourt, Inc. (San Diego, New York and London) (pages from 199 to 204), man lives under two kinds of influences, "Influence A" and "Influence B". There is also a special kind of influence called "Influence C".

"**Influence A**" means worldly influences created in this world, that is, influences of race, nation, climate, family background, education one has, the society one lives in, one's profession, one's wealth, one's poverty, currently prevailing ideas etc.

"**Influence B**" means influences that are created under different laws, that is, esoteric influences, originally created by conscious and evolved beings on this world itself, usually embodied in the form of religious teaching, rituals, philosophical systems, works of art etc, but over a period which have become mixed with "Influence A".

If one is able to differential between "Influence A" and "Influence B", and if one is able to collect and absorbs sufficient amount of "Influence B" by being emotionally touched by it, the possibility of his evolution comes into being in the form of formation of Magnetic Centre (*Khap-Mumukshuta*, a kind of dissatisfaction with ordinary material life and deep desire for evolution) within him; and if the Magnetic Centre is sound and deep enough, it will make him seek right knowledge, right guidance and do right efforts for sufficiently long time.

The existence of seed within one for formation of Magnetic Centre (*Khap-Mumukshuta)* by being touched by "Influence B" may be the result of similar efforts made in past life, or may be a new beginning in this life, or may be because one has somehow at some point of time became useful to some highly evolved person and has earned his good wishes, etc.; there can be many such possibilities but the important point is that if one has Magnetic Centre, then only there is possibility of evolution.

If one is influenced and driven solely by "Influence A" only, then he will not get interested in such knowledge or possibility of evolution even if by chance he encounters it, and therefore, for him there is no possibility of evolution.

It is the beauty of human life that one is absolutely free to choose to make efforts for evolution, or to choose to be fully satisfied with and lead material life only!

"**Influence C**" means a special kind of influence created consciously by evolved being and transmitted directly by means of oral transmission, from one person to another, and which has conscious effect.

Influence of the *Higher Worlds*, *Higher Intelligence* and *Higher Beings* invisibly present right here is another aspect of the "Influence C", that is, the *unknown* factor which is always present *invisibly*.

If one has right knowledge of, and right attitude towards "Influence C"; he experiences and verifies the *touch* of this invisible influence right here, in those moments when one's mind (the Intellectual Centre) is calm and wordless and the heart (the Emotional Centre) is in non-reacting and non-judging state; and feels that somehow "Influence C" is invisibly guiding and illuminating his path of evolution.

Satsang (being in the company) of highly evolved man and the *touch* of "Influence C" both together make one instantly perceive the realness, possibility, and worthy-ness of seeking the evolution.

Naimisharanya Kshetra (The field of higher energy)

Presence of Evolved Man creates certain atmosphere and vibrations around, according to the level of that evolved man's being. Within such vicinity of highly evolved man, Seeker (a person seeking and valuing evolution and loving that evolved man) experiences that the quality of one's attention, the relative silence of the mind and the emotions have become more refined and of different order for the time being. Such field or vicinity of highly evolved man is called *Naimisharanya Kshetra* (The field of higher energy) in Hindu Texts, and being in it is considered to be very conducive for one's evolution.

Certain places of pilgrimage are also considered as *Naimisharanya Kshetra*, for example, certain caves and worship places in the Himalayas.

Scale and Relativity

The concept and the sense of scale and relativity is very important in any field of pursuit. The ***whole*** is made up of various parts and such parts are further sub-divided in to parts of part and so on. In our case the entire scheme of the *Worlds*, that is, the Absolute is the ***whole,*** numerous *World 3*s are its parts, and within one such *World 3*, numerous *World 6*s are parts of part, and so on.

Sense of scale means the understanding that things are placed at different levels, and knowing such various levels in their exact order, with their intrinsic nature and significance. Sense of relativity means the understanding of relative significance of a particular thing in connection with other parts at the same level. The sense of scale and relativity means holistic understanding of scale and relativity put together of the entire scheme of things.

Let us try to understand this by using an allegory: in one Giant Multinational Conglomerate there are many Multi-Products Companies; in each Company there are various Departments like, manufacturing, marketing, accounts, corporate affairs Department etc; and in each Department there are various Divisions like legal, internal audit, finance, taxation etc, in that particular Company's Corporate Affair Department. Various persons heading such Divisions, Departments, Companies and entire Conglomerate have completely different perspective, focus and vision of the entire business empire of that Giant Conglomerate.

If person working in one such division wants to be promoted higher ups to reach the top position, he 1st must broadly understand the hierarchy of positions higher ups, that is, he must understand the scale and relativity of various positions, their qualifications etc. in that Conglomerate. Then he must understand the significance and place of his present job in the Division in which he works, and improve his present work according to its requirements, and then get promoted to head his Division.

Then he must understand the significance and place of the Division which he heads in connection with the Department to which his Division belongs, and improve his work according to its requirement, and then get promoted to head that Department, and so on higher up. The chance of his promotion improves proportionate to the improvement in his understanding of scale and relativity of *scheme of positions* in the entire conglomerate, and on his right efforts.

If he has no knowledge of *scheme of positions* in his Division, in his Department, in his Company, and in his Conglomerate, what chance of promotion he would have, and if by chance he gets promoted one position higher, then also upto how much up he could proceed in his career unless he start having the sense of the scale and relativity and make right efforts?

Non-identification *(Vairagya)*

Non-Identification (which is termed as *Asang* in the Bhagwad Geeta, and as *Vairagya* in *Vedantic* and other Hindu Texts) means not loosing oneself; not becoming one with thought, emotion, impulse, outside object, situation, etc. in question; and in that moment intentionally keeping the sense of Self separate and detached from that thought, emotion, impulse, outside object, situation, etc.

To be identified means in that particular moment loosing oneself; becoming one with particular thought, emotion, impulse, outside object, situation, etc.; and in that moment not having capacity to keep the sense of Self separate and detached from that thought, emotion, impulse, outside object, situation, etc. Further, the identification has degrees, sometimes one is more identified, sometimes less. When we use the word *identifications* we mean one's specific passions (*Ashaktis*) collectively.

Higher Centres (Higher Minds)

There are two Higher Centres (Higher Minds) which man will have when he evolves, the Higher Emotional Centre and the Higher Mental Centre. When one has control over the 3rd state of consciousness, one shall have Higher Emotional Centre, which is the seat of the conscious love, and which can see the connectedness of things.

When one has control over the 4th state of consciousness, one shall have Higher Mental Centre, which is the seat of the objective knowledge (conscious wisdom), and which can see things as they are & can understand the universal laws in operation.

The state of Presence

The moment of presence means, the moments when higher states of consciousness is circulating within one, and one is right here in the moment, and the Higher Centre is manifesting within one. Simply put, the state of Presence means one is right-here *in the present moment* (without thinking about the past or the future) with the presence of Higher Centre (Higher Mind).

Involuntary and mechanical brooding over the past, worries about the future, indulging in the lures that comes one's way during the passage of time, wasting of time in indulging pain avoiding lethargy; and particularly not understanding the intrinsic nature of time, not understanding the value of being right into it, not understanding the possibilities that are lying ahead if one remains in the state of presence for long, and not understanding that still (apart from all these) one can be in the present moment any time if one intends and does right effort and that such state can be prolonged by continuous efforts put in for sufficiently long time; all these make it very difficult and arduous for one to be in the state of Presence. It may be put like:

O lovely Present, ever you come to notice?
So quietly you step that your swift's unseen;
You elude in Past's repent or Future's wish;
O slippery like an eel, against you who can win?

All lures rest in you, only through you they lure;
In your unheeded voyage lures hide their life,
Still leaving your treasure hidden and pure,
O cunning witness of all turbulent strife!

Thinking the best use, O seed of all wealth,
I spent you, ere now, in taking the pain less;
But when I looked for inner shrine where HE dwell'th,
You revealed the secret making me wordless:

> *"True treasure lies in being stilled in Me;*
> *On this lane ahead, lie HIS Home and HE".*

Right now, let us pause for a while, and silently and slowly tell ourselves "I have nothing to think about, nothing to seek, nothing to resent, nothing to *do*, nowhere to go, nothing to gain, just be here". Right utterance of these Work "I"s and simultaneously feeling their meaning within may give us a glimpse of moment of Presence.

Sufi concept of "Smiling forehead"

It is about learning to relax the attention just by effort of trying to feel as if it is relaxing, and when it becomes relaxed and less identified, trying to make it joyful (that is, experiencing the joy right there in consciousness itself, rather than in heart or mind). This will reflect as one's pleasant expressions. Corresponding Hindu concept is of *PrasannChitt.* (*Prasann* means joyful and *Chitt* means attention or consciousness, that is, joyful attention or consciousness). This effort, if rightly done, gives moments of non-identification and the 3rd state of consciousness.

Zodiac Signs & their general affinities					
Sr. No.	**Sign Symbol**	**Western Name**	**Eastern Name**	**Corresponding Body-type**	**Corresponding Center of Gravity**
1		Aries	*Mesh*	Martial	King of Spades
2		Taurus	*Vrishabh*	Lunar-Venusian	Jack of Clubs
3		Gemini	*Mithun*	Mercurial	Queen of Diamonds
4		Cancer	*Kark*	Lunar	King of Hearts
5		Leo	*Sinha*	Venus-Mercury	Jack of Spades
6		Virgo	*Kanya*	Mercury-Saturn	Queen of Clubs
7		Libra	*Thula*	Venusian	King of Diamonds
8		Scorpio	*Vrischik*	Mars - Jovial	Jack of Hearts
9		Sagittarius	*Dhanu*	Jovial	Queen of Spades
10		Capricorn	*Makar*	Saturn-Mars	King of Clubs
11		Aquarius	*Kumbh*	Saturn	Jack of Diamonds
12		Pisces	*Min*	Jovial - Lunar	Queen of Hearts

Note: Here shown is the general affinity of Zodiac Sign with Body-type & Centre of Gravity. One's Body-type depends on the Zodiac Sign that is rising on eastern horizon, and one's Centre of Gravity depends on the Moon's place relative to the rising sign at the time of one's birth. For more details see explanatory notes.

Body-types

There are twelve Body-types, (1) Martial, (2) Lunar-Venusian, (3) Mercurial, (4) Lunar, (5) Venus-Mercury, (6) Mercury-Saturn, (7) Venusian, (8) Mars-Jovial, (9) Jovial, (10) Saturn-Mars, (11) Saturnine and (12) Jovial-Lunar. (Please refer the Diagram of Reflection of Body-type in Eastern Astro Science and the Diagram of Zodiac Signs and their general affinities).

Entire humanity can be divided into these twelve Body-types. Each Body-type has particular psychological characteristics, physical appearance; and affinity with corresponding Essence Activity, Chief-Feature (*Swabhav*) and *Health-Prakriti.*

Certain Body-types are positive type and certain are negative types; and certain Body-types are active type and certain are passive types. Positive type means those types which usually perceive the positive side of the thing, and negative type means those types which usually perceive negative side of the thing, for example, perceiving glass as half filled by positive types, and the same glass being perceived as half empty by negative types.

Active Body-type means those types which mechanically take initiative and work on the situation, and passive type means those types which do not take initiative and mechanically allow the situations to work on him.

Martial is negative active type, Mercurial is also a negative active type but in a different way. Lunar is negative passive. Venusian is positive passive type, Jovial is also positive passive type but in a different way. Saturnine is positive active type. Other types which are having influences of two planets have characteristics of both the planets that combine therein.

The idea of Body-type is dealt with in detail by Rodney Collin in his book *Theory of Celestial Influence* (pages from 143 to 151), published by SHAMBHALA, Boulder and London, 1984, and has shown how various Endocrine Glands work as receiving apparatus for various planetary influences. The idea of Chief-Feature and Body-type has been refined and further developed in the teachings of Robert Earl Burton.

One's Body-type usually depends on which Zodiac Sign is rising in eastern horizon, particularly on the exact point that is rising of that Zodiac Sign at the moment of one's Birth. For example, if the sign Aries is rising in eastern horizon at the moment of one's Birth, one's Body-type usually would be Martial; if the sign Taurus is rising in eastern horizon at the moment of one's Birth, one's Body-type usually would be Lunar-Venusian, and so on.

Body-Types & Processes (*Akarma-Karma-Vikarma)*

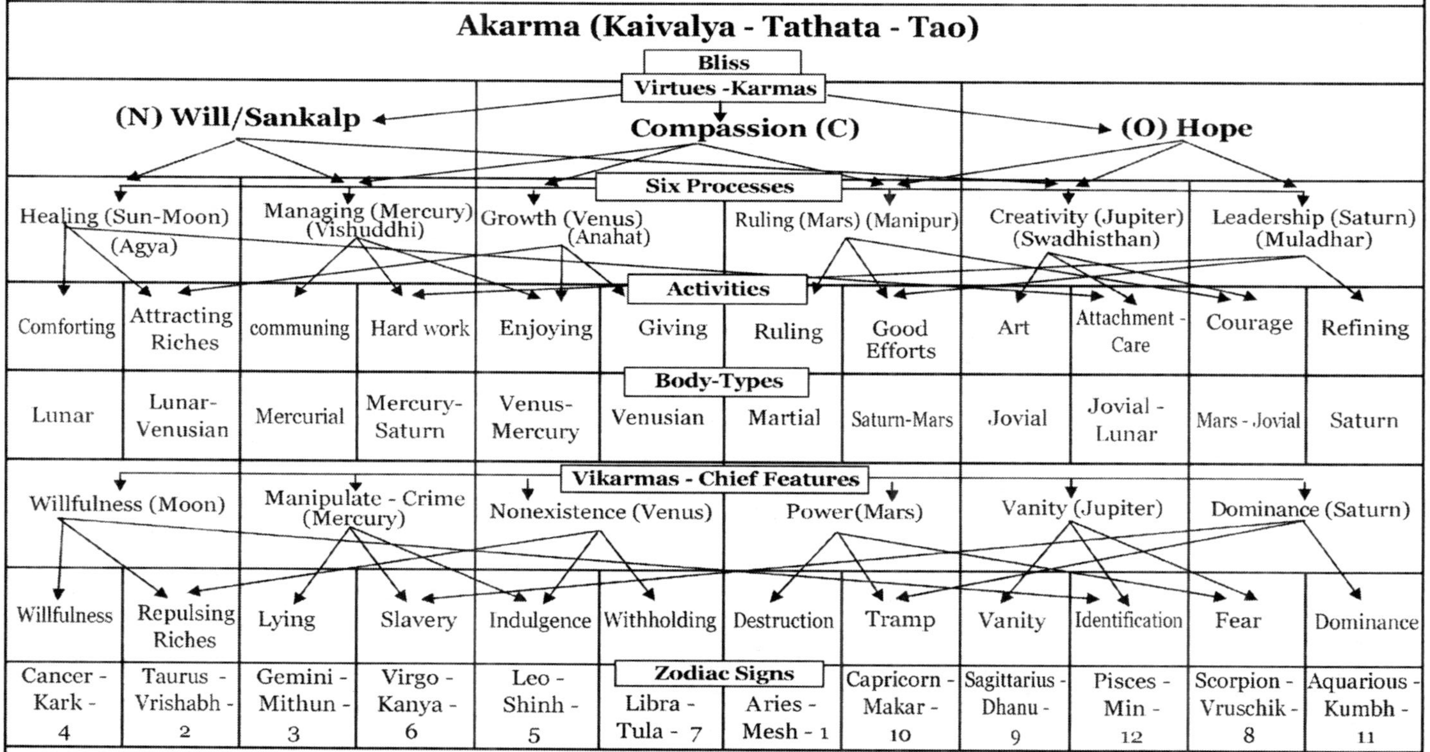

Akarma (Kaivalya - Tathata - Tao)

Bliss

Virtues -Karmas

(N) Will/Sankalp				Compassion (C)				(O) Hope			
Six Processes											
Healing (Sun-Moon) (Agya)		Managing (Mercury) (Vishuddhi)		Growth (Venus) (Anahat)		Ruling (Mars) (Manipur)		Creativity (Jupiter) (Swadhisthan)		Leadership (Saturn) (Muladhar)	
Activities											
Comforting	Attracting Riches	communing	Hard work	Enjoying	Giving	Ruling	Good Efforts	Art	Attachment - Care	Courage	Refining
Body-Types											
Lunar	Lunar-Venusian	Mercurial	Mercury-Saturn	Venus-Mercury	Venusian	Martial	Saturn-Mars	Jovial	Jovial - Lunar	Mars - Jovial	Saturn
Vikarmas - Chief Features											
Willfulness (Moon)		Manipulate - Crime (Mercury)		Nonexistence (Venus)		Power(Mars)		Vanity (Jupiter)		Dominance (Saturn)	
Willfulness	Repulsing Riches	Lying	Slavery	Indulgence	Withholding	Destruction	Tramp	Vanity	Identification	Fear	Dominance
Zodiac Signs											
Cancer - Kark - 4	Taurus - Vrishabh - 2	Gemini - Mithun - 3	Virgo - Kanya - 6	Leo - Shinh - 5	Libra - Tula - 7	Aries - Mesh - 1	Capricorn - Makar - 10	Sagittarius - Dhanu - 9	Pisces - Min - 12	Scorpion - Vruschik - 8	Aquarious - Kumbh - 11

Person having particular Body-Type is likely to have affinity for corresponding Vikarma (Chief-Feature) & Karma (Essence Activity). As his being develops, the grip of Chief-Feature loosens and the corresponding Essence Activity gets strength. Arrows show how basic three virtues combine to produce various activities and how it turns into Feature (*swabhav*) when it degrades.

However, one must verify one's Body-type by self-observation on the basis of reflection of its characteristics, corresponding Essence Activity and Chief-Feature in one's own behaviour over a long period of time. It is a long work and needs patience.

For more details about the characteristics of various Centre of Gravities, Body-types and Features one may refer to the book *Human Types: Essence and the Enneagram* written by Susan Zannos, and published by Weiser Books, York Beach, Me, 1997.

Chief Feature *(Swabhav)*

One's Chief Feature (which is called *Swabhav* in Hindu Teachings) is one's Chief weakness, corresponding to one's Body-type. One has all Features to some extent, but the Chief Feature is one's very nature. Usually one operates between the pendulum of one's Chief Feature and Essence Activity thought out the whole life.

Every one has Chief Feature, some have been given the Chief Feature that is much irritating to, and comes to the notice of, others easily and more often; and some have been given the Chief Feature that is less irritating to, and does not come to the notice of, others so easily and so often; but both are equally a bondage from the view point of the evolution, and on which one has no control at all.

From one angle, if rightly approached and observed, one's Chief Feature is a constant reminder and irritant making one experience one's utter *mechanicalness*; one's always being in bondage created by himself only; and *nothingness* of one's thoughts, knowledge, opinions, *non-realness* of one's emotions etc; and provides the basis for one to look for escape from it, and so, to look for the evolution.

In some cases, the incompatibility and friction of Chief Features between life-partners, if rightly approached, may prove to be a constant reminder for the need to work on oneself. The life of Abraham Lincoln is its glaring example.

One can transcend one's Chief Feature by observing it in oneself, accepting the fact of its existence in oneself, and then slowly and step by step trying to non-identify with it, and thereby separating from it, and then controlling it. Fighting with one's chief feature will not yield any result, as it would mean one feature is fighting with another feature.

Reflection of Human Body-Types, Activities & Health-Prakriti in Eastern Astro Science (Map of the Heavens)

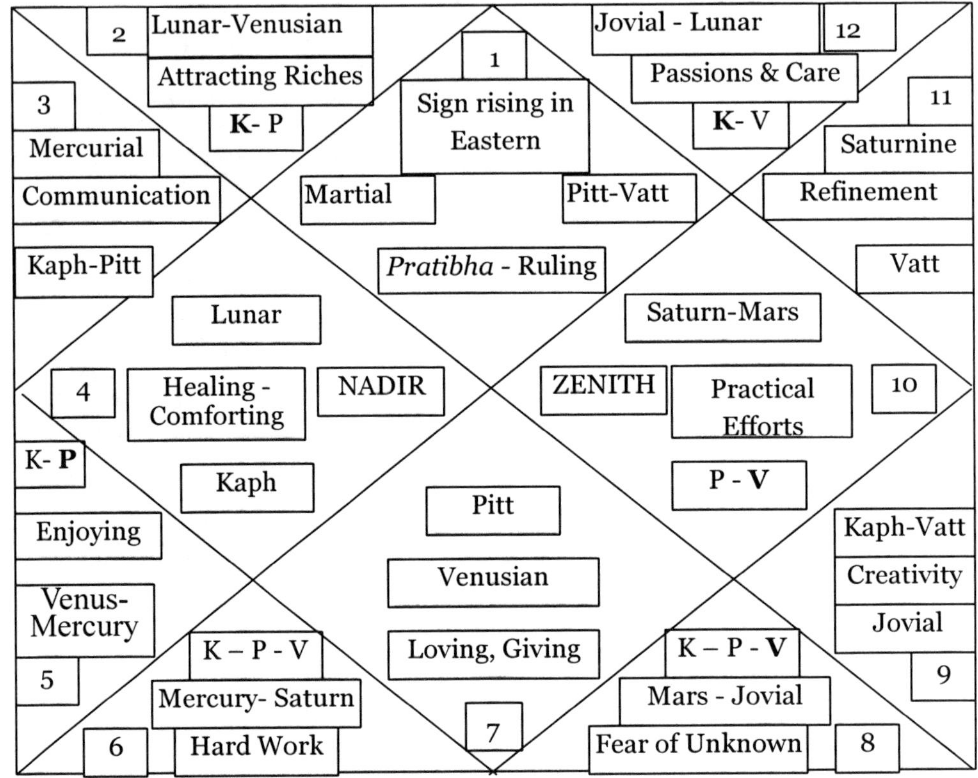

Note: Numbers represent Zodiac Sign No. e.g. 1 = Aries (*Mesh*), 2 = Taurus (*Vrishabh*), and so on. K, P & V are abbreviations for Kaph, Pitt & Vatt respectively, they are shown as abbreviations as they are further dilutions. The bold abbreviated letter shows its relative dominance.

Yes, to rightly work on one's Chief Feature, one need to have sufficient negative attitude (*Shatrubhav)* towards one's Chief Feature, in the sense that one must be convinced by his own experience that it *is* his chief bondage, chief weakness, it has no useful purpose, it is not worth any justification, and that he must transcend it, and eventually destroy it.

Regarding other's features, one need to develop an attitude and understanding that the manifestation of other person's feature is not intentional at al, it is his bondage, he is doing it because he can not help it in the moment; like I have one feature he has another feature. Though such right attitude towards other's feature will not immediately make one to accept other's unpleasant manifestations, it needs long work, but if it becomes one's general attitude, as an undercurrent, it will help a lot over a period.

One can see others according to one's own level of being. While being placed in one's Chief Feature, one can see others as their Chief Feature only. As one develops the ability to observe oneself more objectively (that is, as one really is), one starts seeing others also more correctly. One's approach towards others, and the way one sees others is the index of one's level of being. Only the person who is established in *Atman* (the Spirit) can see all others as *Atmans* (Spirits) or as potential *Atmans* (Spirits).

Body-type Activity and Essence Activity

Body-type activity or Essence activity is one's natural strength, corresponding to one's Body-type. One's Body-type activity and one's Essence activity both are the same but of different quality and at different level.

The Body-type Activity uses ***World 12*** level energy, and in which there is intentionality, non-identified but unified way with unwavering clarity about the purpose and its intrinsic value, and the control rather than pendulum (e.g. like the Kings of Centres - to understand it better by comparison between Kings and Queens of Centres).

The Essence Activity uses ***World 24*** level energy, and which is subject to the pendulum between excellence and Chief Feature (e.g. like the Queens of Centres - to understand it better by comparison between Queens and Kings of Centres)

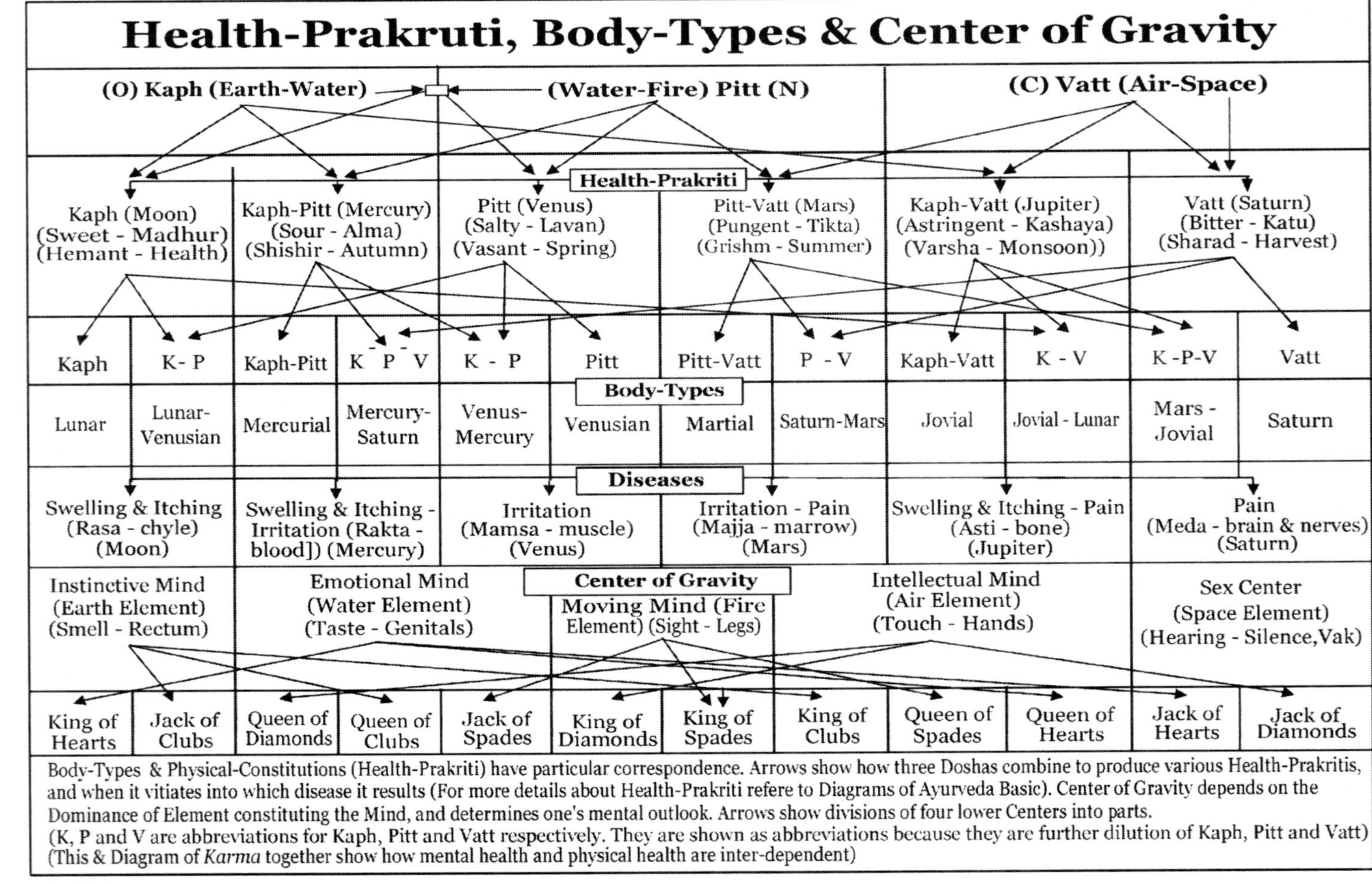

Body-Types & Physical-Constitutions (Health-Prakriti) have particular correspondence. Arrows show how three Doshas combine to produce various Health-Prakritis, and when it vitiates into which disease it results (For more details about Health-Prakriti refere to Diagrams of Ayurveda Basic). Center of Gravity depends on the Dominance of Element constituting the Mind, and determines one's mental outlook. Arrows show divisions of four lower Centers into parts.
(K, P and V are abbreviations for Kaph, Pitt and Vatt respectively. They are shown as abbreviations because they are further dilution of Kaph, Pitt and Vatt)
(This & Diagram of *Karma* together show how mental health and physical health are inter-dependent)

Ayurveda Basics and Health-Prakriti

Ayurveda is an ancient medical science chiefly based on law of three. According to Ayurveda, man's health and physic is made up of three constituent *Dosas* (forces): Kaph (the 2nd force), Pitt (the 3rd force) and Vatt (the 1st force), which are in tern made up of five Elements: Space, Air, Fire, Water and Earth.

One's state of health depends on right balance of these three *Dosas* (forces). In Ayurveda, each food material and herb is classified according to the Elements that food material and herb contains. As these three *Dosas* are made up of various Elements, they can be brought to right balance by intake of right food and herbs containing required Element, and if need be, by abstaining from the certain food that contains Elements which are not good for the balance at the time in question.

As per the Ayurveda, seasons and sub-seasons (Ritus) also plays very important role in the state of the three *Dosas*, and has suggested specific life styles for various seasons and sub-seasons (Ritus).

Health-Prakriti (that is, inborn health Constitution) is a Ayurveda concept and depends on the various six ways in which the three *Dosas* can combine (like the six processes of the three forces), and which have correspondence with Body-types. One's individual Health-*Prakriti* depends on which basic Process or its further dilution is dominant in one, like one's Body-type.

Certain foods, certain tastes and certain herbs are good for certain Health-*Prakriti*, and Certain foods, certain tastes and certain things are not good for certain Health-*Prakriti*. If one knows one's Health-*Prakriti*, and also what is good or bad for one's Health-*Prakriti*, one can use this information for maintaining better physical health.

For knowing more about Health-*Prakriti* and what is good or bad for various Health-*Prakritis*, one may refer to Ayurveda books on this subject (like Charak Samhita, Susruta Samhita, Astang Hridaya Samhita, etc.). The basic attempt here is to show how Ayurveda is based on the Law of Three, and how it is connected with Body-types. The Diagrams of Ayurveda Basic gives overall Ayurveda concept in nutshell; one may go into further details keeping in mind these overall basics.

Law of Three & Ayurveda Basics – 1				
Sr. No.	**Particulars**	**2nd Force**	**3rd Force**	**1st Force**
	Guna	**Tamasa**	**Satva**	**Rajasa**
	Dosha	**Kaph**	**Pitt**	**Vatt**
1	**Outer Form**	**Moon**	**Sun**	**Air**
2	**Properties**	Oily - unctuous (*Snigdha*), Heavy (Guru), Cold (*Sheeta*), Dense, Stable-Static, Slimy-Slippery	Hot (*Ushna*), Sharp (*Tikshna*), Light (*Laghu*), Oily (*Snigdha*), Mobile	Dry-un unctuous (*Ruksha*), light (*Laghu*), Cold (*Sheeta*), Rough, Hard
3	**Functions in body**	Movements of joints, strength, braveness, weight of the body.	Digestion of food, functionality of eye, body colour, hunger and thirst.	Body movements, running, walking, excretion of urine and faeces.
4	**Type of Energy**	Anabolic, Conserving & Stabilizing	Metabolism, Balancing & Transformative	Catabolic, Activating & Dynamic
		It is the energy of Structure	It is the energy of Metabolism	It is the energy of Movement
5	**Effect of deficiency**	It can cause sensation of dryness or internal burning, feeling of emptiness in the stomach and other cavities of the body, looseness of the joints, thirst, weakness, and insomnia.	It can cause dullness of complexion and reduced body heat.	It can cause languor, uneasiness, loss of consciousness.
6	**Effect of excess**	It can cause whiteness of complexion, heaviness of limbs, nausea and fullness of the stomach, feeling of coldness, drowsiness, excessive sleep, and looseness of the joints.	It can cause burning sensation of body, desire for coolness, yellowish coloration (of skin, eyes, feces, urine), insufficient sleep, fainting fits, weakness of sense organs.	It can cause roughness of the voice, thinness of the body, dark complexion, desire for heat, throbbing sensation, hard stool, insomnia, and weakness.
7	**Effect of Vitiation**	It can cause aversion to food, inertness of limbs, vomiting, and impaired digestion.	It can cause heat (fever or hot sensation).	It can cause swelling or distention of the abdomen, rumbling sound of the intestines.

Law of Three & Ayurveda Basics – 2

	Particulars	2nd Force	3rd Force	1st Force
	Guna	**Tamasa**	**Satva**	**Rajasa**
	Dosha	**Kaph**	**Pitt**	**Vatt**
8	**Chief Disease**	Swelling & Itching	Irritation	Pain
9	**Chief Remedy**	Honey	Ghee	Til Oil
10	**Causal Taste**	Sweet, Sour & Salty	Pungent, Salty & Sour	Bitter, Astringent & Pungent
11	**Curing Taste**	Bitter, Astringent & Pungent	Sweet, Astringent & Bitter	Sweet, Sour & Salty

12	**Lower Center**	Instinctive	Emotional	Moving	Intellectual	Sex Center
13	**Corre-sponding Sense**	Smell	Taste	Sight	Touch	Hearing Silence
14	**Corre-sponding Organ**	Anus	Genitals	Legs	Hands	Tongue
15	**Element (Mahab hutta**	Earth	Water	Fire	Air	Space

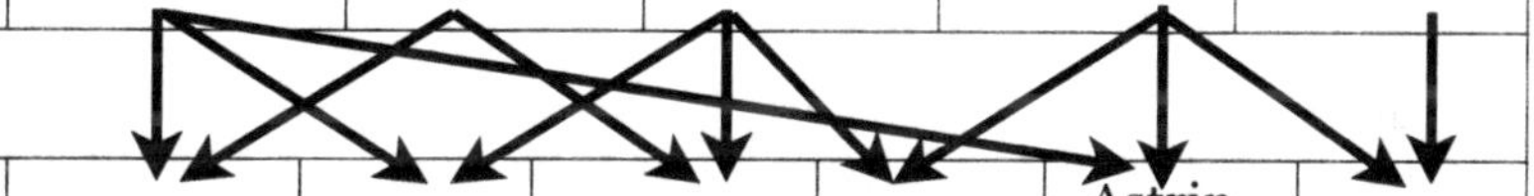

16	**Taste**	Sweet (Madhur)	Sour (Alma)	Salty (La-van)	Pungent (Tikta)	Astrin-gent (Ka-shaya)	Bitter (Katu)
17	**Effects of Taste**	gives cooling effect, increases Kaph diseases and decreases Vatt and Pitt diseases.	gives heat effect, increases Kaph diseases and decreases Vatt and Pitt diseases.	gives heat effect, increases Vatt diseases and decreases Kaph and Pitt diseases.	gives heat effect, decreases Kaph diseases and increases Vatt and Pitt diseases.	gives cooling effect, increases Vatt diseases, decreases Kaph and Pitt diseases.	gives cooling effect, increases Vatt diseases and decreases Kaph and Pitt diseases.

Note: Arrows above show how various Elements combine to produce various tastes, and therefore, which taste is conducive for which Elements.

Law of Three & Ayurveda Basics – 3

Sr. No.	Particulars	2nd Force		3rd Force		1st Force	
	Guna	**Tamasa**		**Satva**		**Rajasa**	
	Dosha	**Kaph**		**Pitt**		**Vatt**	
18	**Health - Prakriti**	**Kaph**	**Kaph-Pitt**	**Pitt**	**Pitt-Vatt**	**Kaph-Vatt**	**Vatt**
19	**Ruling Ritu**	Hemant -Winter	Shishir -Autumn	Vasant - Spring	Grishm -Summer	Varsha -Mon-soon	Sharad -Harvest
20	**Kop (disturbing) Ritu**	Vasant (Spring)		Sharad (Harvest)		Varsha (Monsoon)	
21	**Corre-sponding substance**	Heavy material & Cold Liquid	Hot material	Hot Liquid	Hot Air	Light material	Air & Space
		Heaviness					Lightness
22	**Dhatu**	Rasa [chyle]	Rakta [blood]	Mamsa [muscle]	Majja [marrow]	Asti [bone]	Meda [brain & nerves]
	Psychological equivalent						
1	**Planet**	Moon (Chandra)	Mercury (Buddh)	Venus (Shukra)	Mars (Mangal)	Jupiter (Guru)	Saturn (Shani)
2	**Chief Feature**	Willful-ness	Manipula-tion	Non-existence	Power	Vanity	Domi-nance
3	**Activity**	Healing	Manage-ment	Growth	Ruling	Creation	Refine-ment
4	**Process**	"2-3-1"	"3-1-2"	"1-2-3"	"1-3-2"	"3-2-1"	"2-1-3"
5	**Process Center**	Agya	Vishuddhi	Anahat	Manipur	Swadhist han	Muladhar

Division of Man – Synthesis of 4th Way & Hindu Ideas					
Sr. No.	**World**	***Manas* (Mind)**	***Buddhi - Pragya* (Intelligence)**	***Chitt -Chitti* (Attention - Consciousness)**	***Ahamkar* (Sense of "I")**
1	World 1			*Brahmi* state	*Akshar Brahm*
2	World 3	Higher Mental Centre	Beyond Intelligence	*Kaivalya - Tathata - Tao* (Spirit state)	*Atman* - Spirit
3	World 6	Higher Emotional Centre	Higher Mental Centre	4th State - Objective Consciousness	Real "I"
4	World 12	Unified Mind	Higher Emotional Centre	3rd State - Self-Consciousness	Unity
5	World 24	Balanced work of 4 Lower Centres & Sex Centre	Steward	Controlled & directed but relaxed Attention	Essence
6	World 48	Relatively Right work of 4 Lower Centres	Observing "I" & Deputy Steward	Controlled & directed Attention	True Personality (Magnetic Centre - *Khap*)
7	World 96	Wrong work of 4 Lower Centres	Many "I"s	Fascinated, or very little Attention	False Personality

Division of Man – Synthesis of 4th Way and Hindu Ideas

Know thyself is the basic interest of all esoteric traditions since centuries. Man is divided into various parts. In the 4th Way it is considered that man, as he is ordinarily, can not *do*, everything happens to him; and is a stimulus response machine (that is, man does everything *mechanically* on the basis of accumulated past habits (*Sanskaras*), grooming and make up) which has potential to cease to be a machine, if he realises this fact, and makes right efforts for sufficiently long time under the right guidance.

In the 4th Way man is divided into various divisions according to various view points like False personality (False ego, self-created image of oneself) and "you" (the real substance in one); Knowledge and being; Essence and personality.

False personality means self created image of oneself, based on illusions and misconceived notions; it is one's false ego, as against "you", the real and reliable substance in one. One's Identifications, negative emotions, lies and all hurt feelings are part of his False Personality.

The **Essence** means what one is born with and Personality means what one has learned during the life. For example, one's inherent intellectual capacity is part of the Essence, but the knowledge one has gathered is part of the personality. One's Body-type and Centre of Gravity are part of one's Essence.

The child is in the state of the Essence. The child does things with his entire being, that is, he is wholly in that activity and there is no inner contradiction within him. (by inner contradiction we mean one's inner psychological divisions, that is, one's one part does the activity, another part opposes it, and still another part is indifferent and do not partake in it).

As one grows in age, one learns so many things from the surrounding circumstances, and formation of opinions, judgments, and interpretations starts and in this way the personality comes into existence and eventually grows; and when one's opinions, judgments, and interpretations etc. becomes very much fixed, it is almost the end of any possibility of invoking or developing the Essence.

When one rightly works on oneself and shifts one's focus from other's faults, opinions, comparisons etc. to his own life, likings, valuations, aims etc. his personality starts becoming less insistent. This way one develops ability of bringing the attention back to oneself, the ability to be present to one's own life, and again approaches and eventually enters the state of Essence, and the Essence starts growing and developing. Childlike genuineness and spontaneity is one of the characteristics of the state of Essence.

Right now let us set aside all opinions, thoughts, resentments, judgments, and shift our focus to our own likings, and tell ourselves "There is absolutely no need to take any tension or burden upon myself", and enjoy the beauty of this very moment, which is the core of the life itself. This may give a glimpse of the taste of the state of Essence.

When one works on oneself on right basis and observes oneself, he understands relatively true facts about one's inner life and develops right attitudes towards the life in general, and towards his evolutions and his self in particular. This way one develops **True Personality**. Right attitudes, right knowledge, desire and valuation for spiritual evolution are part of the True Personality. True Personality helps the development of Essence.

Further, in the 4th Way, the MIND is divided into 4 (four) Lower Centres and the Sex Centre. Four Lower Centres are Instinctive Centre, Moving Centre, Emotional Centre and Intellectual Centre.

On the basis of the quality and level of attention, each of these four Lower Centres is further sub-divided into 3 (three) parts namely, intellectual part (working with directed and controlled attention), emotional part (working with attention fascinated and kept by outside object) and instinctive-moving part (working with no or very little attention).

Each of these four Lower Centres is further sub-divided into two halves, positive half and negative half. The positive half of the Emotional Centre is LIKE, and the negative half is DISLIKE. The positive half of the Intellectual Centre is YES, and the negative half is NO. The positive half of the Moving Centre is MOVEMENT, and the negative half is REST. The positive half of the Instinctive Centre is COMFORT, and the negative half is DISCOMFORT. For right orientation in the life both halves are necessary. The Sex Centre has no negative half.

For example, to use positive half of the Intellectual part of the Moving Centre means to MOVE (i.e. to do physical activities) intentionally with full attention, and to use negative half of the Intellectual part of the Moving Centre means to REST intentionally with full attention.

These four Lower Centres and their parts are represented by deck of cards. The Ace of Clubs represents entire Instinctive Centre as a whole, the Ace of Spades represents entire Moving Centre as a whole, the Ace of Hearts represents entire

Emotional Centre as a whole and the Ace of Diamonds represents entire Intellectual Centre as a whole.

The Kings represent intellectual part, for example, King of Clubs represents the intellectual part of the Instinctive Centre. The Queens represent emotional part, for example, Queen of Spades represents the emotional part of the Moving Centre. The Jacks represent instinctive-moving part, for example, Jack of Diamonds represents the instinctive-moving part of the Intellectual Centre. (Please refer the Diagram of Reflection of Centre of Gravity in Eastern Astro Science and the Diagram of Zodiac Signs and their general affinities).

In Hindu Texts man is divided into four *AntahKarans* (Inner Instruments) and ten *BahyaKarans* (Outer Instruments).

Four *AntahKarans* (Inner Instruments) are: (1) *Manas* (the Mind, which is divided into four Lower Centres and a Sex Centre in the 4th Way as discussed above), (2) *Buddhi - Pragna* (Intelligence), the faculty that knows and takes decision. Intelligence is quite different from Intellectual Centre – Intellect - one of the four Lower Centres discussed above, which thinks in verbal terms. The 4th Way equivalent of Intelligence at initial stage is the Steward, (3) *Chitt* (Attention) when develops becomes *Chitti* or *Mahattatva* (Consciousness), and (4) *Ahamkar* (sense of "I", one's self). These *AntahKarans* assume different forms on various levels of evolution as shown in the Diagram of Divisions of Man – A Synthesis of 4th Way and Hindu Idea.

Ten *BahyaKarans* (Outer Instruments) are: five *Gyanendriyas* (Senses: Hearing, Touch, Sight, Taste and Smell) and five *Karmendryas* (Speech, Hands, Legs, Genitals and Rectum). This each pair of five has particular affinity with Elements, four Lower Centres and the Sex Centre.

The Hearing sense and the Speech faculty when it is in silence, have affinity with Space Element and Sex Centre. The Touch sense and Hands have affinity with Air Element and Intellectual Centre. The Sight sense and Legs have affinity with Fire Element and Moving Centre. The Taste sense and Genitals have affinity with Water Element and Emotional Centre. The Smell sense and Rectum have affinity with Earth Element and Instinctive Centre.

Right synthesis of idea of divisions of man as explained in the 4th Way and as explained in the Hindu Texts, give more clear and complete picture of man with his divisions. Most importantly, if one aspires to proceed on the path of evolution, one need to verify for oneself these divisions within oneself by consistent and right self-observation. Please refer to the Diagram of Divisions of Man – Synthesis of 4th Way and Hindu Idea.

Reflection of Center of Gravity & Elements in Eastern Astro Science (Map of the Heavens) & in Deck of Cards

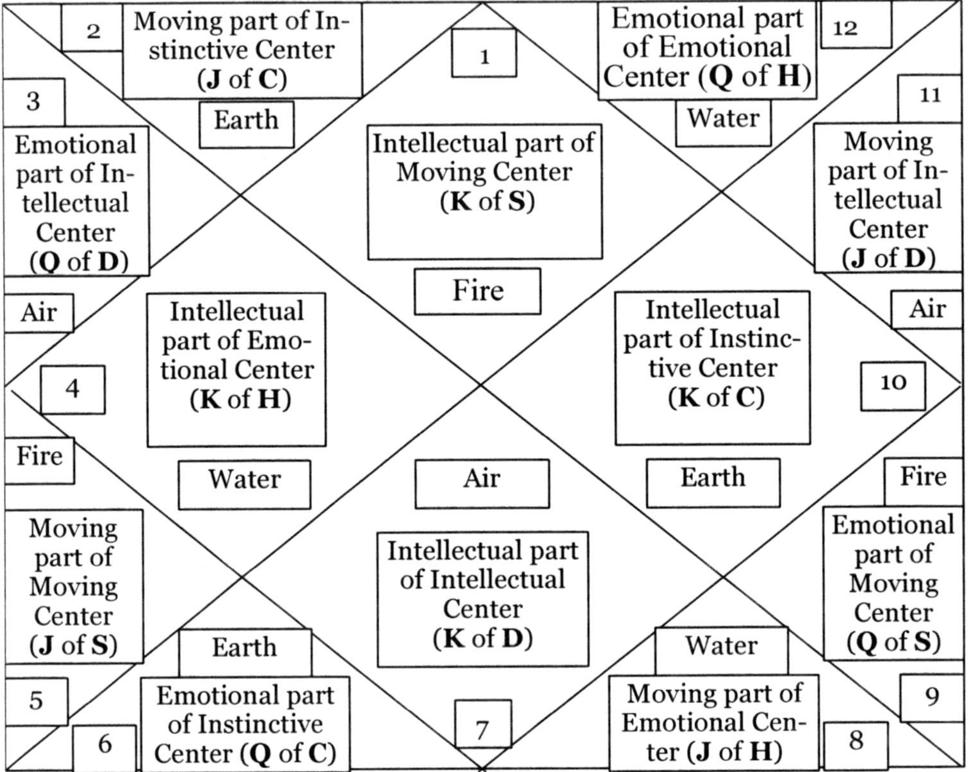

Note: Numbers represents the Zodiac Sign No. e.g, 1 = Aries (*Mesh*), 2 = Taurus (*Vrishabh*), and so on.

K = King, **Q** = Queen & **J** = Jack
H = Hearts, **D** = Diamonds, **S** = Spades & **C** = Clubs
For example, **K** of **H** means King of Hearts

Centre of Gravity

Usually in every person, one part of the one particular Lower Centre is more developed and prominent, and other remaining parts of all four Lower Centres are comparatively less developed. Usually one looks to the world from the point of view of that part of that prominent Centre, which is called one's Centre of Gravity, that is, one's outlook towards the world.

For example, when we say a King of Diamond Martial, we mean, a Martial Body-typed person whose Centre of Gravity is in the intellectual part of the Intellectual Centre. However, as one develops all Lower Centres tends to balance. These four Lower Centres are discussed in detail in the P. D. Ouspensky's books, *The Psychology of Man's Possible Evolution* (Pages from 23 to 30), published in January 1974 by Vintage Books, a Division of Random House, New York.

Usually the Position (*Bhava*) and particularly the exact point of the placement of the Moon relative to the rising Sign in eastern horizon at the time of birth determine one's Centre of Gravity. For example, if the sign Aries (*Mesh*) is rising in eastern horizon at the moment of one's Birth, and the Moon is in Libra (*Tula*), that is, placed in 7th position from the rising Sign, then usually one's Body-type would be Martial and the Centre of Gravity would be King of Diamond.

But if the sign Taurus (*Vrishabh*) is rising in eastern horizon at the moment of one's Birth, and the Moon is in Libra (*Tula*), that is, placed in 6th position from the rising Sign, then usually one's Body-type would be Lunar-Venusian and the Centre of Gravity would be Queen of Clubs, and so on.

However, one must verify one's Centre of Gravity and Body-type by self-observation on the basis of reflection of its characteristics, corresponding Chief-Feature and Essence Activity in one's own behaviour over a long period of time. It is a long work.

For more details about the characteristics of various Centre of Gravities, Body-types and Features one may refer to the book *Human Types: Essence and the Enneagram* written by Susan Zannos (Weiser Books, York Beach 1997).

Human Subjectivity

Man looks at things through the veil or glass of his subjectivity; he can not see things as they really are, particularly in psychological matters. Man can see table as table, in such material things man can see truth or fact as they are, but psychologically each man has his own subjective vision which has very little to do with the truth or fact. The undercurrent of subjectivity prevents man from seeing things as they really are.

For example, Mr. A, a close friend of Mr. B, has brutally insulted Mr. C. Now whenever Mr. C looks at or thinks about Mr. A, the undercurrent of his insult by Mr. A will play a great role; he will assume so many imaginary negative things about Mr. A and so on. But when Mr. B looks at or thinks about Mr. A, he will have completely different perception about Mr. A, as the undercurrent of his close friendship with Mr. A will play a tremendous role in forming his perception or reaction towards Mr. A. In the same way, when Mr. D who has no connection or previous interaction with Mr. A looks at or interacts with Mr. A, he will have completely different way of looking at or reacting with Mr. A.

The whole mass of man's subjectivity is made up of many things like peculiarity of one's body-type, Chief Feature and Centre of Gravity; refinement of one's Essence and Personality; the kind of grooming, culture, education and atmosphere one has been exposed to, kind of people whose company he likes, accumulated past *Karmas* and habits, and such other things. Or in terms of modern psychology the whole accumulated mass of conscious and unconscious mind.

Chief bondage of man is his subjectivity into which he lives and from which he perceives, thinks, feels and reacts throughout his life. This is Maya for him. The real freedom is freedom from this subjectivity, and seeing the truth or fact as it is not only in material things but also in psychological matters.

Spiritual or psychological evolution is first of all realising the fact of this subjectivity in oneself as a matter of fact, observing moment to moment the play of this subjectivity in one's thinking, feeling and reactions, and at the same time not condemning it. And then little by little developing capacity of not identifying with and not believing one's such subjective thinking, feeling & perception as the truth. This becomes possible when one enters the 3rd state of consciousness which is also called as Self-consciousness, i.e. being moment to moment impartially aware of the play of one's own subjectivity.

The crux of the teaching of J. Krishnamurti culminates into moment to moment observing "what is" (he used the word "what is" for one's subjectivity impartially observed without condemnation) and thereby attaining the true self-knowledge, that is, the truth about the self, how it is made up of this subjectivity and so on. And then, trying to see things in the moment, leaving aside one's subjectivity.

True love becomes possible only when one transcends one's subjectivity. After knowing & abandoning one's subjective perception as untrue, the self-inquiry may little by little lead one to the glimpses of the truth. Ramana Maharshi taught the method of self-inquiry by asking within, "Who am I?". One can see things objectively, that is, things as they really are, in the 4th state of consciousness.

Properties of various States of Consciousness			
Sr. No	**World**	**State of Consciousness**	**Properties**
1	World1	*Brahmi* state	*Brahmrup* state; ineffable, beyond all relativity; merges his *Atman* in *Brahm*; alone knows truth in its full sense
2	World3	Spirit state	*Kaivalya* state; conscious (*Shakshi*-witness) of *Shushupti* (dreamless sleep); able to measure all and encompass all
3	World6	4th State - Objective Consciousness	Bliss state; fully objective towards whatever one observes; conscious (*Shakshi*-witness) of dreams; exalts in flow of esoteric knowledge and attains equanimity
4	World12	3rd State - Self-Consciousness	*Shakshi-Bhava* state, Divided attention state; fully objective towards oneself; conscious (*Shakshi*-witness) of waking state; obtains whatever one desires, and becomes the prime.
5	World24	2nd State - 3 Dimensional relaxed Attention	Waking state (psychological sleep) but with child-like spontaneity, and relatively frequent glimpses of 3rd State.
6	World48	2nd State - 2 Dimensional Attention	Waking state (psychological sleep), with glimpses of Essence & of 3rd State.
7	World96	2nd State - 1 Dimensional narrow Attention	Waking state with rare glimpses of Essence & of 3rd State in exceptional moments - in highly emotional states, in moments of danger or beauty, in very new and unexpected circumstances and situations. (1st State is biological sleep, and 2nd State is psychological sleep)

Note: Normally one can have glimpses of next higher state of Consciousness, but one can not have glimpses of higher than the next higher state of Consciousness, e.g. when one is in the 2nd state one can have glimpses of 3rd state, but can not have glimpses of 4th state; and due to any reason if one have, one can not remember or understand it.

Level of Being

The level of being means the degree of spiritual evolution one has attained, and which reflected in: (1) the degree of Non-Identification (*Vairagya,* non - attachment) with one's desires, passions, illusory sense of *doing* and senses indulgences (2) degree of control achieved over the self, that is, self-observation of one's Chief Feature (*Swabhav*), acceptance of it without inner argument or justification, separation from it, and then transcending it (3) the state and the degree of consciousness acquired. Broad characteristics of various level of being (evolution) are shown in the Diagram of The Ladder of Evolution.

Without the growth of level of being, no amount of knowledge can help, as it would turn into mere confusing information without the sense of its inter-connectedness, relativity and scale. Understanding is combined result of knowledge and being. Understanding grows only with the growth of being. Understanding is the result of participation of two or more Lower Centres on the same subject at the same time. In the process of living, one's level of being changes moment to moment.

Man No. 1 means an ordinary man whose Centre of Gravity is in the Moving or Instinctive Centre. Man No. 2 means an ordinary man whose Centre of Gravity is in the Emotional Centre. Man No. 3 means an ordinary man whose Centre of Gravity is in the Intellectual Centre. From the point of view of the level of being and evolution Man No. 1, 2 and 3 are placed equally.

Man No. 4 means a man who has Magnetic Centre (*Khap-Mumukshuta*) and his primary focus is on work (*Sadhana*) and who's 4 Lower Centres are more or less balanced. Man No. 5 means a man who has control over the 3rd State of Consciousness and has Higher Emotional Centre (the seat of conscious love), and can see the connectedness of things.

Man No. 6 has 4th State of Consciousness and has Higher Mental Centre (the seat of the Objective Knowledge). The Objective Knowledge means knowledge of things as they really are and ability to see and understand universal laws in operation. The chief difference between Man No. 6 and Man No. 7 is that, in man No. 7 it has become permanent, but in Man No. 6 it has not become permanent, and he can lose it.

States of Consciousness & Depth of Awakening					
Sr. No	**World**	**State of Consciousness**	**Mandukya Upanishad Description**	**Depth of Self-Remembrance & Awakening**	**Quality of seeing oneself**
1	World1	*Brahmi* state	4th Quarter - *Brahm* itself	Remembrance of one's Existence & Oblivion, both	As the Galaxy sees him
2	World3	Spirit state	3rd Quarter of *Brahm-Pragya*	Remembrance of one's entire Existence as a whole	as the Sun sees him
3	World6	4th State - Objective Consciousness	2nd Quarter of *Brahm-Taijasa*	Remembrance of one's entire Eternity as a whole	as the Earth sees him
4	World12	3rd State - Self-Consciousness	1st Quarter of *Brahm-Vaisvanara*	Remembrance of one's entire Life as a whole (Time Body)	as Nature sees him
5	World24	2nd State - 3 Dimensional relaxed Attention		Relatively Coherent Remembrance (closure to sub-conscious)	as other Man sees him
6	World48	2nd State - 2 Dimensional Attention		Relatively Momentary Remembrance	in self-created Image (with glimpses of 5 above)
7	World96	2nd State - 1 Dimensional narrow Attention		Momentary Remembrance – vivid & alive memory of few exceptional moments only	seeing oneself entirely in self-created Image

The Ladder of Evolution					
World	**Level of Evolution (Being)**	**Chief Law operating (H)**	**Psychological equivalent of respective World's own additional three Laws**		
			(N)	**(C)**	**(O)**
Param Brahm					
World1	Man No. 9	*fana* in *Brahmic* devotion	*Brahmi* State		
World3	Man No. 8	*Kaivalya* - *Tathata* - *Tao*	*Purush* - *Kaivalya*	*GunSamya Prakriti* - *Maya*	*Kal* - Time - Existence (Space)
World6	Man No. 6 & 7	Law of Will (Inner & Outer)	Purest *Satva* *Purn Gyan Shakti* - Objective Consciousness	Purest *Rajasa* *SatyaSankalp*- Conscious wish	Purest *Tamasa* *PurnKarya Shakti* - Miraculous Ability to Do
World12	Man No. 5	Law of Will (Inner)	Conscious Love & Con-science	Will - Ability to Resolve	Self - Rememberence & Unity
World24	Man No. 4	Law of Fate (Law of Types) (Tendencies of Past Actions)	Faith with Understanding	Permanence of Tendency	Care - Sensitivity
World48	Man No. 1-2-3 with Magnetic Centre (*Khap*)	Law of Cause & Effect	Focused/ Controlled Attention	Magnetic Centre (*Khap*) - Desire	Identification Mechanicalness (Chief Feature)
World96	Man No. 1-2-3	Law of Accident	Rules - Imposed Discipline	False Ego - Craving - *Vasna*	Ignorance - *Mudhta* (utter Mechanicalness) (Mere Chief Feature)

Note: Without the guidance of Man No 5, 6 or 7, it is almost impossible to proceed rightly on Evolution. The grace of Man No 8 or 9 can make the Crystallization (*Nirvikalp Nischay*) happen in a sufficiently prepared and open man if he has unquestioning love for that Man No 8 or 9. The Ladder of Evolution proceeds upward from bottom to top.

Man No. 8 means a man who has attained the State of *Atman* (the Spirit) and who is beyond Higher Centres and Higher Self. Man No. 9 means a man who is established in *Brahmi* State (the state of the Absolute), and has sublime devotion and servitude towards THE ALMIGHTY.

The quality and connectedness of one's knowledge depends on his level of being. One can understand things according to one's level of being, for example, what Man No. 6 or 7 can understand practically, may only be a *Philosophy* for Man No. 1, 2 or 3, and may only be a *Theory* for Man No. 4 or 5.

What one can understand and can do practically, we may call it *Practice*. What one can not understand fully and can not practically do, but can calculate and can make exact road map out of it to proceed on, we may call it *Theory*. What one can not calculate and can not understand theoretically also, but which attracts his heart, we may call that it is a *Philosophy* for him.

If rightly approached, the *Philosophy* can provide a broad direction like the North Pole does in the mid Sea, the *Theory* can serve as road map to be used to reach to a definite destination, by practically applying the tools and methods that one can really *Practice*.

By honest self-observation one must verify one's own level of being on right basis; being true to oneself is the basic and foremost requirement for spiritual evolution. One can start only from the place one is actually standing upon. No journey can start from the imaginary place.

As one evolves, he moves up on the ladder of evolution and progressively attains the level of being from Man no. 1, 2, 3 to Man No. 4, then Man no. 5 and so on. As one evolves, what was *Theory* previously may become *Practice*, and what was *Philosophy* previously may become *Theory* for him.

Level of Evolution & Degree of Immortality					
Sr. No.	**World**	**Level of Evolution (Being)**	**Corresponding Body & Mind (H)**	**Degree of Self-Mastery**	**Degree of Immortality**
1	World1	Man No. 9	*Brahmic*	Beyond *Akarma*	Imperishable (*Akshar*)
2	World3	Man No. 8	*Atmic* - No Mind	Creation & Realization of New Possibility (of *Akarma*)	Within limits of our Galaxy, Milky Way
3	World6	Man No. 6 & 7	*Vigyan* (Causal)- Higher Mental	Realization of all Possibilities (Ability to Do - *Siddhis*)	Within limits of our Solar System
4	World12	Man No. 5	Astral (Subtle) - Higher Emotional	Realization of 1 Chief Possibility (by *Non-Doing* the Chief Feature)	Within limits of our Earth
5	World24	Man No. 4	Gross - 4 Lower Centres & Sex Centre (Right work of Centres) - Essence	Creation of Tendency of Realization of 1 Chief Possibility	Possibility of attaining relative Immortality
6	World48	Man No. 1-2-3 with Magnetic Centre (*Khap*)	Gross - 4 Lower Centres & Sex Centre - True Personality	Unrealised Possibilities	Infinite Births & Deaths
7	World96	Man No. 1-2-3	Gross - 4 Lower Centres misusing Sex Energy - False Personality	Spoilage of Unrealised Possibilities	Infinite Births & Deaths

Degree of Immortality

Degree of Immortality means ability to sustain consciousness of the Self and corresponding higher body even after the death of the physical body to the point and degree indicated against the respective level of being (evolution) in the Diagram of Level of Evolution and Degree of Immortality.

For example, Man No. 7 is immortal within the limits of our solar system, it means, in Man No. 7 the Consciousness is crystallised with the material of our Galaxy, the Milky Way, and so, within the limits of our solar system nothing can de-crystallise it. However, in the event of destruction (*Pralaya*) of our entire solar system, his consciousness of self, and so, his immortality will end.

But for an ordinary un-evolved man, on death of the physical body, the consciousness of self ends and assumes the form of seed. In the next life everything is new for him as though occurring for the first time, and the cycle of such births and deaths goes on endlessly.

Manifestation of energy of various Worlds in human actions

When one does something in a reactive way, with negative emotions immersed in one's action, or to show off, that time it is reflection of *World 96* energy working in him. All the expressions of negative emotions, too much identification, *formatory* thinking, criminal activities, etc. are the expression of *World 96* energy.

When one does something with full and controlled attention, with practical thinking and right attitude, that time it is reflection of *World 48* energy working in him.

When one does something with refined emotional element added to it, with right sensitivity, enjoying the action itself, that time it is reflection of *World 24* energy working in him. Heart touching poetry, fine works of art etc, is the expression of *World 24* energy.

When one does something intentionally, in non-identified but unified way, with divided attention, with unwavering clarity about the purpose and its intrinsic value, that time *World 12* energy is present in it. It is doing things with presence, the 3rd state of consciousness.

Quality of Impressions (Hydrogen) & their effects					
Sr. No	**World**	**4th Way Description**	**Corresponding Impression - (*Hydrogen*)**	**Effect of Impression (*H*) on Man**	**% in Man**
1	World1	The Absolute	Hydrogen 1 = Man no. 9's Grace	*Uttam Nirvikalp Nischay*	0.78
2	World3	All Worlds (All Galaxies)	Hydrogen 3 = Man no. 8's Grace	Crystallization – *Nirvikalp Nischay*	1.56
3	World6	All Suns (Our Galaxy) (Milky Way)	Hydrogen 6 = Bliss, Ecstasy	Glimpses of Objective knowledge	3.12
4	World12	Our Sun (Solar System)	Hydrogen 12 = Love, extreme Beauty, etc.	Glimpses of Non-Identification, Freedom, love, etc	6.25
5	World24	All Planets (Planetary Sphere)	Hydrogen 24 = Nature's Beauty, True Friendship, fine works of art etc.	Glimpses of Spontaneity, Innocence, Poise, Happiness, feeling at home etc.	12.50
6	World48	Organic Life on Earth (the Nature)	Hydrogen 48 = Plain Space, etc	If absorbed, Ascending Impression Octave begins	25.00
7	World96	Moon	Hydrogen 96 = Negativity, Depression, Violence etc.	If absorbed, Descending Octave of Degeneration, Crime, Disease etc. begins	50.00

Note: % in the last column indicates the usual proportion in normal ordinary human being. As one evolves the proportion of finer energy increases and that of grosser energy decreases, rather, one's evolution depends on production & retention of finer energy, and transformation of grosser energy into finer energy within one's organism.

Impressions *(Tanmatras)*

When one indulges in the foods through five senses with *identification* (attachment) it is called *PanchVishaya* (five sense indulgences). But when one learns to absorb the finer aspects of the foods through five senses without reacting to them, without identification with them, and with relaxed and divided attention, it becomes Impression (*Tanmatra*, the term used in Hindu Texts), and the Impression octave begins producing higher and finer energies in one's organism.

Tanmatras (Impressions) are the core subtle Elemental (Hearing, Touch, Sight etc) aspect contained in gross sense objects. When we *hear* sounds with relaxed and divided attention without reacting or judging it, allowing it to fall upon us; that time it becomes and enters as *Tanmatra* (Impression) of the Space Element in our organism according to that particular sound's inherent quality.

When we *Touch* something with full heart, with relaxed and divided attention without reacting or judging it, allowing it to penetrate us; that time it becomes and enters as *Tanmatra* (Impression) of the Air Element in our organism according to that particular thing's inherent quality.

When we *See a* particular sight as a whole by focusing on *in-between space*, with relaxed and divided attention without reacting or judging it; that time it becomes and enters as *Tanmatra* (Impression) of the Fire Element in our organism according to that particular sight's inherent quality.

When we *Taste* the food with relaxed and divided attention, experiencing its taste without *identification*, with the presence of the Self detached from the indulgence of the food; that time it becomes and enters as *Tanmatra* (Impression) of the Water Element in our organism according to that particular food's inherent quality.

When we *Smell* something without *identification,* with relaxed and divided attention, experiencing the smell touching the nostrils; that time it becomes and enters as *Tanmatra* (Impression) of the Earth Element in our organism according to that particular smell's inherent quality.

Apart from the fact that whether Impression (*Tanmatra*) is being indulged or absorbed, they have inherent quality of their own. Some Impressions inherently have high quality, like a beautiful sight of the Nature, feeling of true friendship, love etc. and produces quite different effects on us.

Apart from these Elemental *Tanmatras* (Impressions), there exist the Impressions of Higher *Worlds* as well, which touch and enter into us through non-resenting Emotional Centre, Sex Centre and Higher Centres in their respective order, for absorbing which different kind of efforts are required. However, beyond certain point of evolution, right Impressions enters into organism just by intention, without any other efforts. The nature of Impressions of various *Worlds* in order of their level is shown in the Diagram of Quality of Impressions (Hydrogen) and their effects.

Hydrogens

When we say *Hydrogen 12*, on material side we mean the basic material energy unit of *World 12*, that is, atomic energy; and on psychological side we mean the Impression on the level of *World 12*, that is, conscious love, extreme beauty, etc., or energy of *World 12* level produced and present in one's organism.

In the same way, when we say *Hydrogen 24*, on material side we mean the basic material energy unit of *World 24*, that is, molecular energy; and on psychological side we mean the Impression on the level of *World 24*, that is, Nature's beauty, true friendship, fine works of art etc., or the energy of *World 24* level produced and present in one's organism.

On psychological side Hydrogen and Impression both mean the same thing. Intake of higher hydrogen (higher impressions) result into production of better and finer energy within our organism.

In connection with the three forces, as such Hydrogen does not carry any force; but when it combines with the active charge it becomes Active force (C), when it combines with the passive charge it becomes Passive force (O), and when it combines with the neutralising charge it becomes Neutralising force (N).

For example, C = Heat, O = Flour, N = Water and H = Bread. The Bread as such does not carry any force, but for very hungry person it acts as *Active force*, enticing him for eating it; in connection with a person whose stomach is full, when offered it acts as *passive force*, creating resistance in him for eating it; and for another person when it is eaten in combination with pickle, cooked vegetable etc, it acts as *Neutralising force*, by enhancing and balancing the overall taste.

Further, Hydrogen (H) is the result of unification of the three forces of immediate higher order. For example, *Hydrogen 12* is the result of unification of *Carbon 6, Oxygen 6 and Nitrogen 6*. When *Hydrogen 12* carries Active force it becomes

Carbon 12, when it carries Passive force it becomes *Oxygen 12* and when it carries Neutralising force it becomes *Nitrogen 12*. And when *Carbon 12, Oxygen 12 and Nitrogen 12* unify together it results into Hydrogen of next lower order, that is, *Hydrogen 24*. In the same way when *Carbon 24, Oxygen 24 and Nitrogen 24* unify together it results into *Hydrogen 48*, and so on.

Human Organism and various grades of energies (Hydrogens)

The subject of how the organic food that we eat, the air that we breath and the impressions that we take in, enter and digest in our organism; and how the higher and finer energies can be produced in our organism has been discussed beautifully and in much detail by P. D. Ouspensky particularly in Chapter 9 (page 167 to 198) of his book *In the Search of the Miraculous,* published by Harcourt, Inc. (San Diego, New York and London).

Various grades of energy (Hydrogen) is produced in our organism by digestion of different kinds of foods that we take in. Certain portion of the energies produced in this digestion process is consumed in certain human activities and remaining portion proceeds on for further refinement as below:

Hydrogen 96 H96 is animal magnetism and plays very important role in human life, and it is used in the process of attractions and repulsion in interpersonal relationships. If one always remain fascinated in this activity or frequently come under the influence of repulsive relationships, H96 get consumed in large quantity leaving less for further digestion.

However, H69 can be used intentionally and productively by spending certain time, without fascination, with the people with whom one feels friendly and nourished (because when people who are friendly with each other meet without fascination they mutually enrich each other with H96).

Hydrogen 48 H48 is one's thought, if one spends it in constant and uncontrolled day-dreaming and imagination, one feels exhausted and less of H48 will remain for further digestion. Exactly this happens with ordinary man, he is always engrossed in unnecessary regrets about past happenings or negative imagination about the future.

H48 can be fruitfully used in useful intentional thinking on desired subject. This will enrich one's mental life and one can have much useful knowledge.

Normally the impressions that enter human organism through the senses are of the level of H48. Impression of level of H48 is plain like blank sheet of paper. When the Impressions fall upon one's senses, one immediately react to it by thinking about it, speaking about it or expressing like and dislike about it. This will prevent the further digestion of that Impression, and at the same time it is wastage of H48 present in one's organism.

If one can take in Impression, that is, intentionally notice it without inner verbalization and without inner reaction towards it, then the digestion of Impression octave proceeds further and the Impression taken will be digested for further refinement. And this is one of the most important aspects of one's work.

Hydrogen 24 H24 is the emotional energy (both pleasant emotion and unpleasant emotions), and also that energy by which our instinctive and moving centre work. If one spends it in expressing every unpleasant emotion and every unpleasant sensation that may arise, one will be left with very less of it for the further digestion, and at the same time one will always feel the insufficiency of it for other useful functions in one's psychological life and for one's physical health.

When one uses H24 for instinctive and moving functions one remains healthy. But when one is performing physical activities heedlessly and in lethargic manner, it means one is using H48 instead of H24, and this is one of the reasons for physical ill health.

The speed of H24 is said to be 30000 times higher than H48, and because of that only we are not able to notice our emotions as easily as we notice our thoughts. Further, if one has enough H24 one remains perceptive and feels full of energy and one's interpersonal life will be rich.

And this receptiveness will help in taking in better Impressions and also in further development of Impression octave. When one notices fineness in the Impression, for example, the beauty of the Nature vividly that means either the Impression of the level of H24 has entered one's organism, or the Impression H48 taken in has been digested to become H24.

Hydrogen 12

H12 takes three forms in human organism, (1) Sex energy, (2) feeling of quite distinct and light sensation about oneself and (3) finer and higher emotions and higher understanding.

Intense negative emotions also contain H12 in it. The speed of H12 is said to be 30000 times higher than that of H24, and because of that only we are not able to stop the expression of intense negative emotions. The sex centre works with H12. Higher emotional centre also works with H12.

H12 is used healthily in normal sexual life. But its wrong uses must be understood properly. This is the finest energy that is produced in ordinary healthy human organism.

The wastage of this energy takes various forms. When it is misused by Emotional Centre, it takes the form of unnecessary vehemence in emotions and is expressed in behaviour showing constant excessive attraction and engrossment towards opposite sex. The fine energy of H12 is misused by eyes also, when one is looking at person of opposite sex in very fascinated way with an undercurrent of intense sexual attraction. The expression of negative emotions like, anger, irritation, jealousy, self-pity, etc is the biggest misuse of H12.

Real and higher order of work on oneself starts by minimizing the misuses of H12. When one realises the truth of this in oneself, he understands why he should not express negative emotions, and what he loses by expressing it. Over a time, with diligent efforts, he will be able to find ways of not expressing it. And eventually he will be able to transform negative emotions by not identifying with it.

When properly canalized, H12 become creative energy and manifest in artistic creation. When H12 is transmuted into the

Astral body, it reflected in third state of consciousness, unity of the four lower centres, and positive emotion of conscious love and compassion. On mental plain it becomes higher understanding expressed in ability to see connections between the things, which are otherwise impossible to be noticed.

Hydrogen 6 H6 reflects in the forth state of consciousness, and in ability to see and understand the universal lows by which things are connected and governed, and also in ability to see thing as they are.

Human Organism is like an instrument which can use different grades of fuel and can produce results according to the quality of fuel being used in the moment. It is like a burner having connection with 5 tanks of different fuel (H96, H48, H24, H12 and H6) and each fuel having right use. For thinking it needs burning of H48, for interpersonal relation with fine emotion it needs H24 and so on. But if one tries to feel with H48, or if one tries to think with H24 it will be the use of wrong energy and will produce bad results.

Usually the human organism of ordinary man have various proportions of various energies, lower grade energies are more and finer grades of energies are less (For usual proportion of various grades of energies in ordinary human being, please refer to the Diagram of Quality of Impressions and their effects).

When one indulges in excessive smoking (or chewing tobacco or other such habits), alcoholism and drugs like marijuana etc, it is like forcefully squeezing finer energies (the proportion of which is already very low at bare minimum level to sustain good health of the organism) from one's organism and making it available for burning to produce artificially the elating state for self-indulgence at the cost of one's physical and psychological health.

Thereafter it takes time for organism to recoup such loss or damage; however, certain damages caused by such consistent misuse may never be recouped later. Smoking, etc squeezes H24, alcoholism squeezes H12 and drugs like marijuana, etc squeezes H6 from the organism and make it available for burning to provide the *kick*.

The many "I"s

Any chaotic thought, emotion or instinctive-moving impulse that emanates from the *mechanical,* stimulus response and lower aspect of one's being - *World96* and *World 48* is called Many "I"s.

Work "I"s

Well understood and deeply felt powerful short thought, uttered and instructed to oneself is called Work "I". For example, when in the moment one observes that his mind is occupied with unnecessary thinking on a particular subject, and instructs oneself by uttering inside "I have nothing to think about", and if the thinking about that subject completely stop, then it means that one has successfully used it as Work "I"

Initially utterance of Work "I" may seem not working, but, if practiced whole heartedly over a period, little by little it will start giving results.

Vikarma

All mechanical actions coming from False Personality, inherent tendencies of Essence, and all mechanical actions coming from Chief Feature or other Features are called *Vikarma.*

Karma

Actions that come from Non-doing Chief Feature, all actions coming from Law of Will, and at its highest degree all actions coming from *Siddhis* (miraculous ability to do) and virtues, are called *Karma.*

Akarma

Actions that come from Non-doing *Siddhis* (miraculous ability to do), and all actions that come from operating under the Law of *Tathata* (*Kaivalya*), and all actions the fruits of which has been rightly abandoned are called *Akarma.*

Types of *Karma/Vikarmas*

The *Karma/Vikarmas* are of three kinds: *Sanchit, Prarabdha* and *Kriyaman.* The *Kriyaman* is our daily ordinary activity what we normally call in our daily life, as action.

The *Sanchit* is accumulation of effects of our daily actions which we have performed in the past (and in the past lives uptill now) and still which has not (but is in the process of, depending upon its intensity and its repeated nature), touched & became part of our inborn basic nature, our deepest self, the root place where the karmic effects accumulates and reinforce or modify or annihilate the existing cause, or create the new cause. (Which G. I. Gurdjief and P. D. Ouspensky called **Essence,** in the Bhagavad-Gita and other Hindu Texts what is called **Prakriti,** and what modern psychology tries to describe, however insufficiently - not covering its all aspects, as **Subconscious** mind).

The *Prarabdha* is the effects of past actions that has, over a period of time or lives, penetrated into the **Essence** and has created permanent tendency in it and which is now shaping one's life by giving results. The *Prarabdha* determines one's fate.

How action becomes *Karma-Vikarma*

Having understood the **Essence** and **Personality**, we need to understand the significance of above three types of *Karma/Vikarmas* in the process of formation and shaping of one's fate. And also, to understand the science of *Karma* it is important to understand the significance of the fact whether one is established in Personality or near the Essence or in the Essence while performing the Action.

(When one realizes and feels with one's deepest and entire being the significance and truth of the theory in question, is can be said that one has understood it. Such understanding gives freedom and ability to put the idea into practice according to its right significance, or rather, appropriate actions take place from such understanding.)

When one is established in Personality, where man normally does, and performs action, one is far from the Essence and its effects rarely touches the Essence. However, every action is in a way a cause and has an effect. The actions repeated over a period of time forms habits and little by little, if it acquires permanency its effects may create the possibility of touching the Essence. The effects of such *Kriyaman* accumulate and become *Sanchit*.

When one is established near the Essence, where man sometimes in deep emotional moments does, and performs action, its effects may touch and influence the Essence. The effects of such *Kriyaman* accumulate and become *Sanchit*, which has the possibility of becoming the *Prarabdha* in comparatively lesser time.

But when one is established in the Essence or is in moments of conscience, where man rarely does, and performs action, its effects do penetrate and influence the Essence. The karmic effects of such *Kriyaman* accumulate and reinforce or modify or annihilate the existing cause, or create the new cause in the Essence. It is the *Kriyaman*, which has immediate and direct effect on *Prarabdha* and the fate.

The strength, type and quality of one's Essence determine his tendencies, interests and quality of his Personality and consequently his inner conditions. At the same time, his state of being in the moment and his inner conditions do have effect on his Essence. The essence is connecting link between man and Higher Forces. The Essence is the place from where issues the materialization of one's fate.

One's fate, one's life depends upon his past and present actions. As one cannot undo his past actions, one has the only option, that is, to try to see and understand what one can do now, today by his present actions.

Life & Death

To understand the death one need to understand the process of biological sleep (1st state). When we go into the biological sleep, what happens? At the end of the day when we enter into biological sleep, our entire body and our lower centers (conscious mind) enter into rest state, and we (lower centers & conscious mind) forget our Identity and our existence. In the morning, when we wake up again from biological sleep, we experience that our body is refreshed, our lower centers are refreshed, our memory & sense of identity returns.

The death is an analogous process but on a bigger scale. The biological sleep is on the scale of a day within overall period of life span. The death is on the next higher scale, that is, on the scale of a life-span within overall period of eternity (repetition of lives).

In the death process we leave the physical body and our Essence (and sub-conscious mind) enter into oblivion (i.e. higher and next dimension of biological sleep), and the Essence forgets all the memory & Identity of the present life. When we get re-birth after the period of oblivion (like we wake up in the morning after biological sleep on day-scale), we get new body, new lower centers, new life span etc, according to the overall quality of tendencies accumulated in our Essence, which may get modified at the end of each life span depending on one's efforts for evolution and other *Karmas*. Our lower centers (conscious mind) & Identity enters into new cycle afresh for this new life-span.

Seen from larger perspective, as the biological sleep is refreshing, rest giving to our physical body and lower centers (conscious mind) at the end of the day, likewise the death is rest giving to our Essence, and gives us new physical body and new life-span. So, one need not be afraid of the death that comes in the natural course of the things.

What we see as our life is the process of coming together & sustaining together of the physical body, Essence (Essence is the seed-form of all *Karmas* & tendencies inseparably clustered around the Spirit, the *Atman*) and *Prana* (finer *Jad-Chidatmak* energy, what we call the life-force).

The *Prana* keeps the physical body and the Essence together in alive state. By the right and sustained efforts for evolution chiefly by way of transmutation of sex energy, intense negative emotions & suffering, the *Prana* gets refined and crystallizes into Astral Body.

When the *Prana* still gets further refined chiefly by annihilation of ego (me-ness, the lower self) through special kind of effortless-ness, that is, abandoning of doership – sense of doing, it crystallizes into *Vigyan* body (Electron body). This is next higher level of effort and must not be confused with passivity or our ordinary concept of letting things to happen.

When ordinary human being dies, the *Prana* (finer energy, the life-force) leaves the physical body and goes to feed the Moon, that is, it gets absorbed into the self-feeding & self-sustaining mechanism of the Cosmos, and the Essence goes into oblivion state. In this process all three, i.e. physical body, *Prana* and Essence lose *aliveness*.

But when evolved man in whom the Astral body is crystallized dies, his Astral body (along with the consciousness of the self) survives after the death of his physical body till the existence of our Earth. When man in whom the *Vigyan* body is crystallized dies, his *Vigyan* body (along with the consciousness of the self) survives after the death of his physical body till the existence of our Solar System. And so on for man evolved still further. The Astral Body, etc. (along with the respective consciousness of the self) disintegrates at the end of the life of the Higher Cosmos up to which one's immortality extends, and one again enters the cycle of birth & death.

Section II: Enneagrams & Processes

Orders of Laws and Enneagrams

The Enneagram is a pictorial way of showing simultaneously the inter-relation between the operations of three forces, six processes and resultant twelve Body-type activities. In Enneagram the pyramid is made up of three forces, six outer points are the six processes, and twelve lines joining one process with another are twelve Body-type Activities. The quality of three forces determines the quality of six processes and resultant twelve activities.

The three levels (3, 6 and 12) represented in Enneagram are three orders of law in overall scheme of *Worlds*, and within particular *World* as well. If we put entire scheme of laws in one Enneagram then, pyramid represents ***World 3*** level, Six process points represent ***World 6*** level, and twelve joining lines represent ***World 12*** level. At ***World 3*** level, 3 forces are in theirs purest and highest form; at ***World 6*** level, six processes are in their purest and highest form; and at ***World 12*** level, twelve Body-type Activities are in their purest and highest form.

Enneagram also shows what quality of six processes and twelve activities that respective *World*'s own 3 new laws will produce.

For example, when one is operating from ***World 12*** energy, that time his own 3 forces (*Satva, Rajasa* and *Tamasa*) are 3rd state of consciousness, will over his own manifestations, and unity in his behaviour. These 3 forces will combine and accordingly corresponding quality will reflect in six processes; and his Body-type Activity will manifest in its pure form, i.e. he will have control over his own Essence Activity, chief feature and other features.

When one is operating from ***World 24*** energy (the Essence), that time his own 3 forces (*Satva, Rajasa* and *Tamasa*) are his faith (self-belief) with understanding, permanent tendency of his Essence reflected in his body-type, and a kind of sensitivity and emotionality in his behaviour. These 3 forces will combine and accordingly corresponding quality will reflect in six processes, and he will excel in his Essence Activity.

When one is operating from ***World 48*** energy (True personality), that time his own 3 forces (*Satva, Rajasa and Tamasa*) are his controlled attention, desire (magnetic centre, if one has), and his chief feature. These 3 forces will combine and accordingly corresponding quality will reflect in six processes, and his chief feature and other features will reflect in his behaviour.

Enneagram: 4 States of Energy/Matter – Active (C), Passive (O), Neutralising (N) & the Unification of 3 (H)

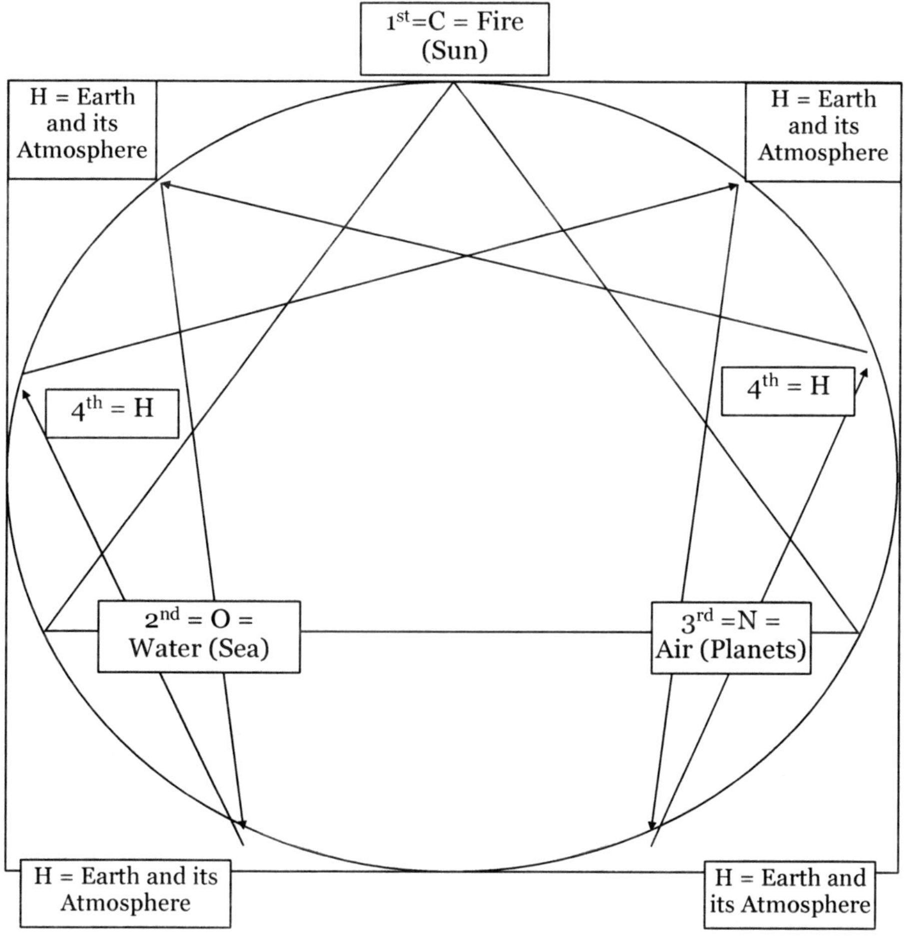

Enneagram: Essence Activities & Chief Features of Ordinary Man

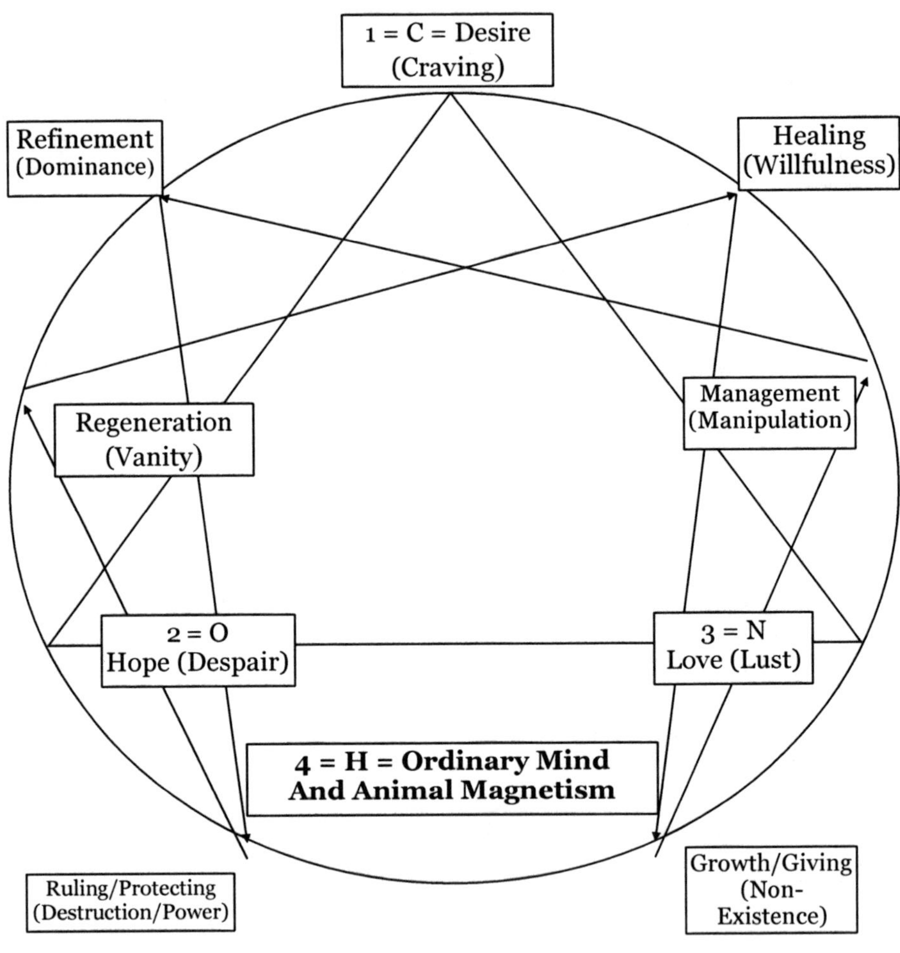

Enneagram: Activities of Evolved (Conscious) Man

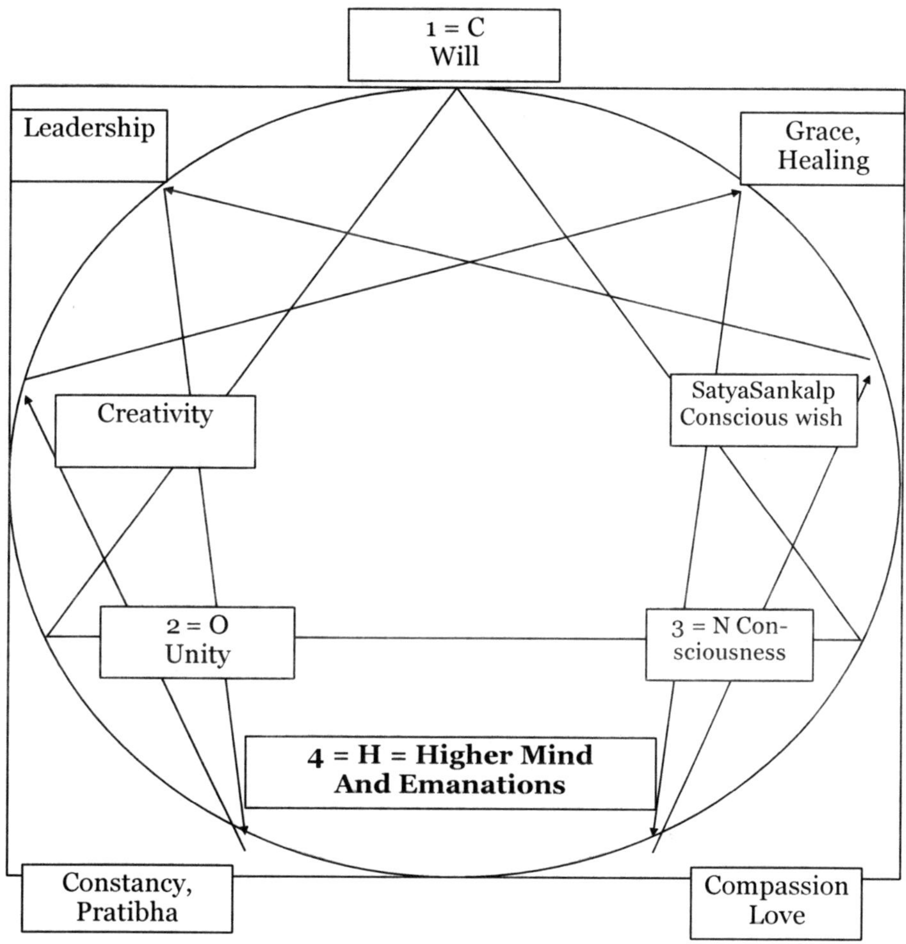

Enneagram: Entry of Triad for perpetual occurring of 6 Processes (Law of Three & Law of Seven operating simultaneously)

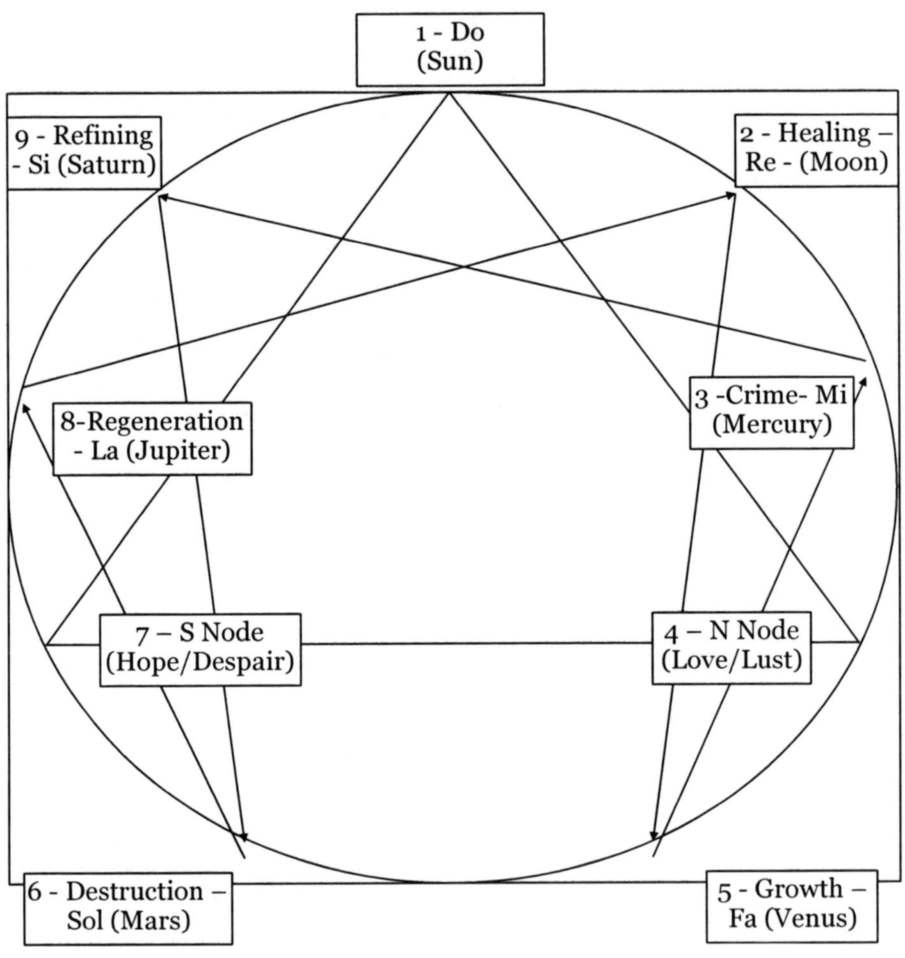

Enneagram: 3 Seasons, Unification of 3 (H) and 6 Ritus – sub seasons. (Law of Three & Law of Seven operating simultaneously)

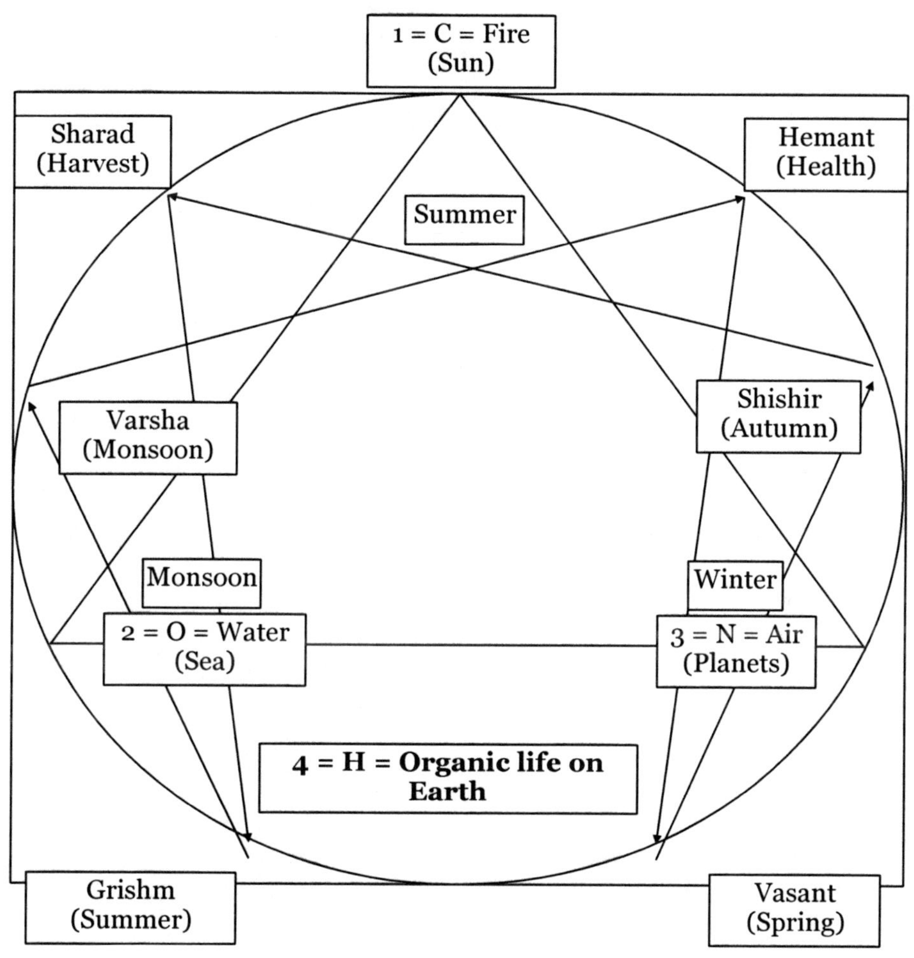

Enneagram: Entry of Higher Triad for Health by 6 Tastes (Law of Three & Law of Seven operating simultaneously)

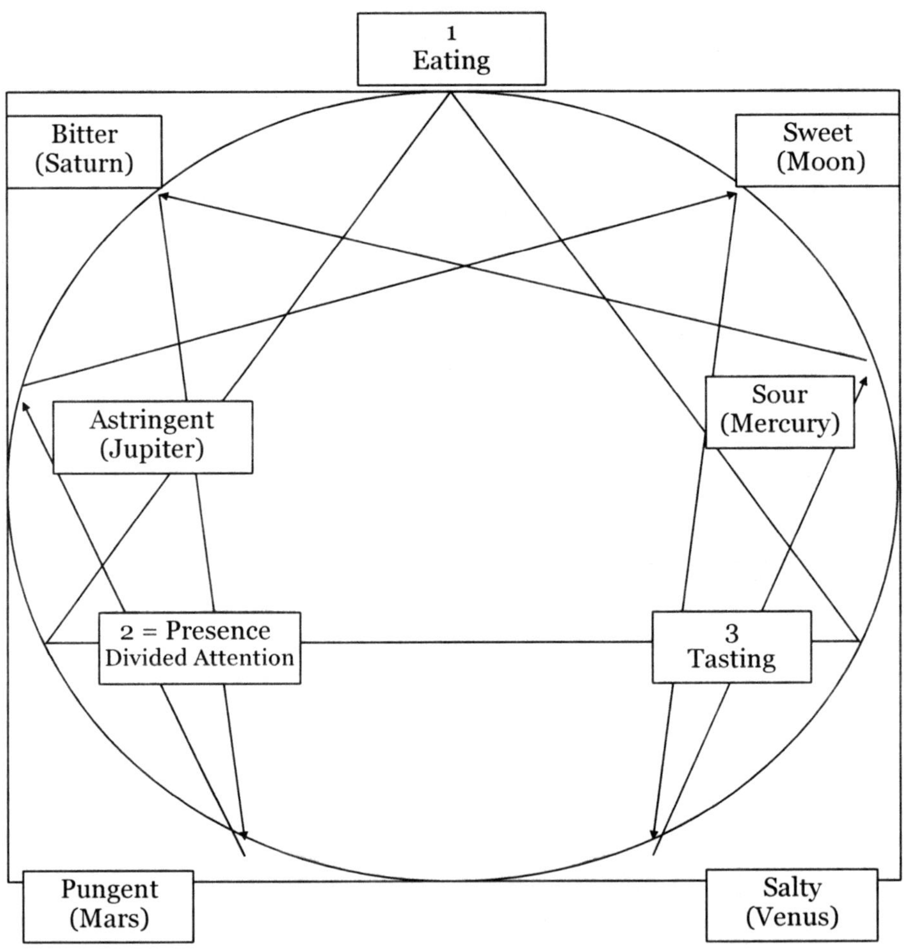

Enneagram: Entry of Triad & occurrence of Six types of Chemical Reaction (Law of Three & Law of Seven operating simultaneously in Chemistry)

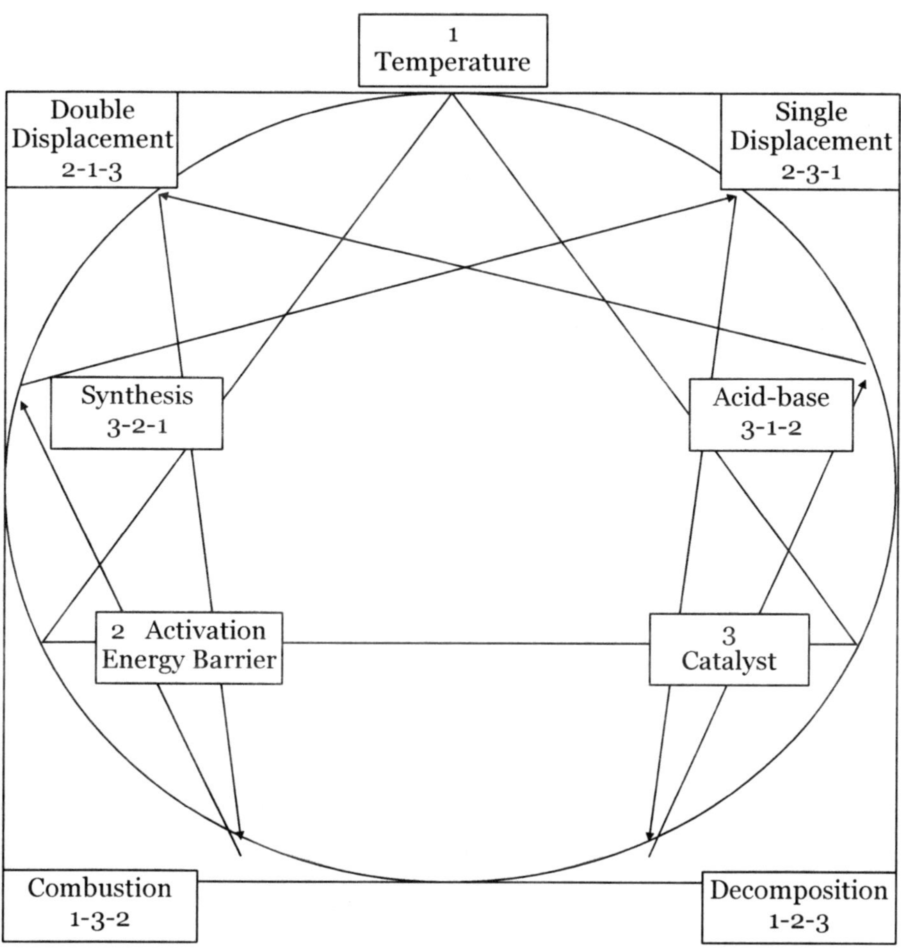

Enneagram: Musical Notes (Octave) (Law of Three & Law of Seven operating simultaneously in Music)

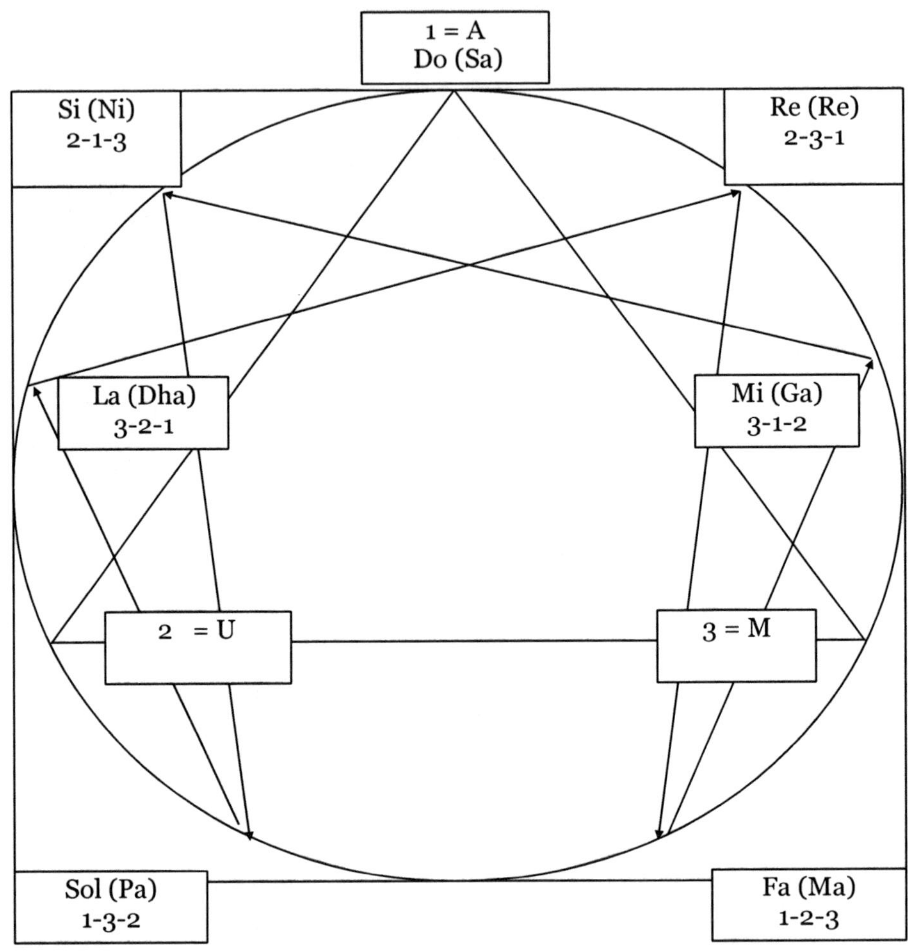

AUM is one syllable world, and is the basic sound. It has three components A, U & M, which represents basic trinity of sounds, from which all other musical notes emanate.

Location of Process Points in human organism			
Sr. No	**Process**	**Location**	**Description of *Chakra* (Process Point)**
1	*Sahastrar Chakra*	**Top of the Head**	The name of this sublime Chakra (Centre) is *Shahshtrar*, the seat of the Spirit, if activated connects one with the Absolute and THE ALMIGHTY.
2	*Agya Chakra* Healing (2 - 3 - 1) (Sun & Moon)	**Forehead**	Its name is *Agya Chakra* (Command Centre), as the *Agya* (inner command) issues from here. It is the seat of the Higher Self & Will. When the brilliance of the Sun combines with the soothing & healing qualities of the Moon, *Agya Chakra* becomes operative.
3	*Vishuddhi Chakra* Manipulation (3 - 1 - 3) (Mercury)	**Throat**	Its name is *Vishuddhi Chakra* (Purification Centre), as it is the centre where crime and negative emotions neutralize & transform. It is the seat of the Essence. It is located at the place from where words arise, and so, it is the seat of silence as well.
4	*Anahat Chakra* Growth (1 - 2 - 3) (Venus)	**Chest**	Its name is *Anahat Chakra* (Centre of *Anahat* -uncreated voice). It is a place from where unconditional love flows, and so, one need not do its verbal expression, as love has its own silent language, which is heard by the hearts of others, and thus growth flowers on its own.
5	*Manipur Chakra* Destruction (1 - 3 - 2) (Mars)	**Solar Plexus**	Its name is *Manipur Chakra*. Manipur means a city of gems. When tremendously destructive power is channelized for the higher purpose, it produces the riches & beauty like that of a city of gems (*Manipur*).
6	*Swadhisthan Chakra* Regeneration (3 - 2 - 1) (Jupiter)	**Navel**	Its name is *Swadhisthan Chakra* (Centre of especial abode of the Lower self). When the Lower self is transformed, it creates the freedom and space for the regeneration.
7	*Muladhar Chakra* Digestion (2 - 1 - 3) (Saturn)	**End of Spinal Cord**	Its name is *Muladhar Chakra* (Basis Centre). When things are digested & refined rightly, it creates the sound basis and foundation for something new & higher.

Helpful Work "I"s for actualisation of various Processes

3 - 2 – 1 (Regeneration-Creativity; Jupiter) Give (feeling joy of giving); nothing to do, no where to go, just being here; observer & observed is one; no negative belief for anyone; "I am, here"; letting *Chitti* (finer) impressions to fall upon & absorbed through *Swadhisthan Chakra*. (If rightly done, all these Work "I"s make one to experience the free-self, and attract good luck.)

1 - 3 – 2 (Ruling-Cleansing; Mars) Not considering; no negative imagination; feeling good about & respect for one's being, abilities, etc; intentionally using King of Spades in physical activities; trying to be conscious while walking; "I can do, invisible Powers are with me"; letting *Chitti* (finer) impressions to fall upon & absorbed through *Manipur Chakra*. (If rightly done, all these Work "I"s make one *Pratibhasampan* (awesome), and give one the ruling power.)

2 - 1 – 3 (Refining-Digestion; Saturn) intentionally hoping, and keeping one's hope touching the ground of *Muladhar*; while being in despair, "let it happen, let me study it"; "I hope, better"; letting *Chitti* (finer) impressions to fall upon & absorbed through *Muladhar Chakra*. (If rightly done, these Work "I"s make one to really receive the fruits of one's efforts, and give one the leadership qualities.)

3 - 1 – 2 (Management; Mercury) Keeping the mind sited upon the place from where words are arising; and intentionally wishing thing to happen and simultaneously, disregarding all apparent facts that are against that wish, as **HE** has all the powers & knowledge; and during all that while feeling head, forehead & naval relaxed, together; "I wish bliss"; letting *Chitti* (finer) impressions to fall upon & absorbed through *Vishuddhi Chakra*. (If rightly done, all these Work "I"s give one the ability to wish consciously)

1 - 2 – 3 (Growth; Venus) No more cheating; trying to understand other's stand; not judging, feeling that judging or mending others is not my job, HE is the best judge; not wishing anyone's harm or degradation; enjoying the voluntary sharing of happiness with others; feeling friendship, respect & love for others; "I love all"; letting *Chitti* (finer) impressions to fall upon & absorbed through *Anahat Chakra*. (If rightly done, all these Work "I"s make one to attract love and riches.)

2 - 3 – 1 (Healing; Moon) Making *Sama* (relaxed & cool) head & forehead; "let it be healed"; letting *Chitti* impressions to fall upon *Sahstrar Chakra, Agya Chakra* & all around head and face. (If rightly done, this helps healing ill situations.)

All these Work 'I's are relative to the Body-types, and their effectiveness depends on its right uttering & simultaneously feeling deeply the meaning behind that particular Work 'I'. To understand this aspect better, please refer to the Diagram of Location of Process Points in human organism.

Section III : Practical Work *(Sadhna)*

Higher method of learning

Possibility of right understanding increases if from the very inception one keeps in mind that whatever one is studying is connected to so many other things and to the ***whole*** in a definite manner. Initially this idea serves as thin guideline only, but as one is able to connect more and more things together in a definite way the idea of the whole stats unfolding.

This process would evoke the use of three Lower Centres simultaneously on the same subject: (1) the intellectual part of the Intellectual Centre, as it would require controlled and directed attention of the King of Diamond (2) the intellectual part of Moving Centre, as the visualisation aspect of the King of Spade of keeping in mind the picture of whole and relative place and significance of parts in that whole is involved and (3) the intellectual part of the Emotional Centre would be evoked by the resultant *appreciation* of the profound and valuable aspect touching one's own evolution.

Using two or more Lower Centres on the same subject at the same time would result into it becoming part of one's lasting and *alive* understanding.

Apart from the above, one should also keep another very important point in mind that our thinking mind, that is our intellect, has definite limitations and it alone on its own can not experience a new phenomena. Yes, it can describe in verbal terms the experience, perception or glimpses of higher Intelligence that one has. When the thinking mind is in relatively silent and calm state, possibility of receiving higher perception opens up.

One may read and study the available material on particular subject in above manner, and then keep aside whatever one has gathered on that subject, to keep the mind silent, open and unbiased; and then clearly formulate a question and honestly pose that question to oneself internally like, for example, *"What this means to me? What is its true significance?"*, knowing well that at present I do not know the real answer but the answer can unfold if I let myself be silent, and let the higher influences to penetrate. In other words, it would be like letting the meaning to unfold from within.

This process will make that question as a silent undercurrent within one's Essence, and would attract the right influences and situations for the answer to unfold. Perceptions after such honest self-inquiry enters in our that *part*, that is, in our consciousness, which understands things without words, and becomes part of our permanent understanding. Probably, following reflects one of the ways in which such understanding could occur:

When I pray to have strength in my heart
To play life's role as does the actor in Play;
That's like, a child who's cleaned a piece of art
And hopes to have a crown of gold as pay,

Or a student who has just started to learn
And hopes to do what his master can not!
O naïve heart, discern this, and it do earn
By labor of love, "What's the worth of mere thought?"

But, tonight thou wert mad in a mystic mood,
Gavest me in such careless drunkard state
A key, "Don't try too hard and also don't brood,
Let my glimpse emerge that'll open all gate.

I love him, who's conscious of his smallness,
And still doesn't pity it - that's real greatness."

Blending of the Law of Three and Triguna (Satva-Rajasa-Tamasa)

The Law of Three Forces is one of the fundamental law governing the Universe and Man, and is a chief constituent of the whole web of Maya. In man's psychological side it reflects as *Triguna* (*Satva, Rajasa* and *Tamasa*) i.e. consciousness (attention in ordinary man), will (desire, craving and restlessness in ordinary man), and self-remembrance and unity (lethargy, delusion and ignorance in ordinary man).

When the three forces combine in various ways, it creates six processes, which reflect as six distinct kinds of activities in man. When it descends further, it reflects as one's fixation in one of the twelve Body-types. When it descents still further, it reflects as fixation in one's Essence Activity and Chief Feature corresponding to one's Body-type (Please refer to the Enneagram of Essence Activities and Chief Features of ordinary man).

When it descends still further it reflects as one's Centre of Gravity (mental outlook). When it descends still further it reflects as one's negative emotions and utter mechanical-ness. And as the ordinary human psyche is usually made up of whole web of these descended laws (Maya), man's behaviour reflects Essence

Activity (fine emotions), Chief Feature, fixed Centre of Gravity, negative emotions, etc. simultaneously in a complex way.

In the 4th Way, the dynamic aspect of three forces has been focused more, i.e. more focus is on the process of combining of the three forces, and its consequences, rather than their exact essential nature and psychological characteristics.

In the *Sankhya* Hindu Texts, and in Chapter XIV of the Bhagwad Geeta their exact psychological nature and essential characteristics: what makes it occur, its reflection in human psyche, its consequences, and its remedial tools are focused more, rather than in what it will reflect when their combining descents further.

In the 4th Way, its dynamic aspect, i.e. way of their taking each other's place, and its mechanism of combining has been explained in much profound and practical way. In the Hindu Texts, their psychological characteristics, its causes and remedial aspect has been explained in much deeper way.

First, one may study and try to understand both separately without mixing one with another as if they both are not connected at all, i.e. forgetting one completely while studying the another, and grasp the crux of the both separately.

Then, one may allow the connection of both of them to unfold step by step, and try to understand that certain aspects are more profoundly explained in one, and certain in another; how they complement each-other; its practical implications; and then, one may do well to blend them both together as one principle, and apply it practically.

Practical work on Satva, Rajasa and Tamasa (three forces)

One may try to work practically on *Satva* (the 3rd force), *Rajasa* (the 1st force) and *Tamasa* (the 2nd force) within oneself in following way:

Rajasa's inherent nature is its intense activeness, such activeness which has much intensity but less sustenance (to use Physical science allegory we can say, electromagnetic waves with very high frequency but of very short wavelength, like ultraviolet waves and X-rays, not visible but its effects can be felt).

The reason for this restlessness is the intensity of the identification with the outcome expected of that particular thing. Craving is its good example. Craving means much too identification with what one wants. If it comes to one's observation and understanding that this very intensity of identification with results is becoming the hurdle in achieving it, and if one learns and tries to reduce that identification, then craving assumes the form of desire.

And if the identification is completely done away with in the moment, still keeping the energy involved in tact, it becomes conscious wish, and probability of its actualisation increases many fold. (Like in our allegory, taming and using otherwise very harmful X-rays for the benefit of humanity).

When this effort of non-identifying is made, *Rajasa* (1st force) is made to occupy the 3rd place (even though inherently it has the 1st place), like in regeneration process (3-2-1). If rightly done, it becomes the process of conscious wishing. G. I. Gurdgieff said, by conscious wishing anything can be achieved.

In *Satva,* there is non-identified dynamic clear energy, consciousness, and ability to see and know rightly (in our allegory, it is like electromagnetic wave with frequency and wavelength both at mid range that is visible to eye, *conscious*), But, in us the quantity of this energy is less, and moreover, non-initiative-taking being this energy's inherent nature, it manifest rarely in us in normal course.

So, one can try to make it initiative taking by making effort to be *Present*, and thereby increase its volume as well. Inherently *Satva* has the 3rd place, but by making effort to be present in the moment in action, one is making it to occupy the 1st place, like in regeneration process (3-2-1).

In *Tamasa,* there is lethargy and inertia (like in our allegory, electromagnetic waves with much too long wavelength but much too law frequency, like radio waves, which neither can be seen nor its effect can be felt in normal circumstances), one can try to put more and more efforts consistently, disregarding "I"s about its uselessness. However, the Lower self will bring forth such "I"s to keep its lethargy in place.

Rightly working on *Tamasa* would have effect of bringing our densely mechanical and unconscious part to consciousness - visibility. (like in our allegory, using radio waves by tuning TV Set to view instantly the things that are happening far away).

Inherently *Tamasa* has the 2nd place (as much inertia is in it), but, when we put energy consistently in some work which is desirable but we have lethargy and dislike for doing that, then it results into the 2nd force occupying the 1st place, like in refinement process (2-1-3).

KarmaYoga (being present while in action)

KarmaYoga (that is, being present while in action) has various facets. (1) The identification with the outcome that is expected of the action in the moment (2) the psychological burden of past actions, working as undercurrent in the moment (3) and the pressure and tension of the course of actions that are yet to take place are the chief obstacles for *KarmaYoga* (being present while in action) and makes one lack the freedom and spontaneity.

The efforts of non-identifying in general (and particularly at the time of speaking or communicating), that is, purifying *Rajasa* by making it occupy the 3rd place, like in 3-2-1, is the work on above 1st obstacle.

Abandoning the fruits of one's past actions by knowing and feeling that I have never *done* anything, everything has happened due to the operation of the three forces, and I am separate and detached from all the three forces, one can work on above 2nd obstacle.

Learning to willingly leave things on the intelligence of "Influence C" is work on the above 3rd obstacle. This is transcending one's *doership* (illusory sense of doing), and is quite different from passive Body-type approach of not taking initiative. By consistence practice of these three tools, one learns to slowly move from *Vikarma* to *Karma* and eventually to *Akarma*.

Verse II – 50 of the Bhagwad Geeta says, "The person whose *Buddhi* (Intelligence) is rightly placed is he who set aside the identification with both bad and good Actions (both, *Vikarma* and *Karma*). And so, establish yourself in *Yoga* of not identifying with both bad and good Actions, for such *Yoga* is the excellence in action (*Yogah Karmeshu Kaushalam*), in other words, such *Yoga* would result in the excellence in action."

***Patanjali AstangYoga* & the 4th Way**					
Sr. No.	**World**	**4th Way Equivalent**	***Patanjali Yoga* Tool**	***ChittVriti* (Attention - Consciousness)**	**Sense of "I"**
1	World 1				
2	World 3	Dying to *Siddhis* & Higher Self	*Kaivalyam - Nirbij Samadhi*	*Kaivalya - Tathata - Tao* (Spirit state)	*Atman* - Spirit
3	World 6	Dying to Lower self, and Acquiring Miraculous Abilities (*Siddhis*)	*Samadhi & Saiyam*	4th State - Objective Consciousness	Real "I"
4	World 12	Sustaining Presence & 3rd state	*Dharna & Dhyan*	3rd State - Self-Consciousness	Unity
5	World 24	Work on Emotional Centre & the Essence	*Pranayam & Pratyahar*	Controlled & directed but relaxed Attention	Essence
6	World 48	Creating Moon in one-self	*Ashan*	Controlled & directed Attention	True Personality (Magnetic Centre - *Khap*)
7	World 96	Good Householder Discipline	*Yam & Niyam*	Fascinated, or very little Attention	False Personality

Patanjali AstangYoga and the 4th Way

Maharshi (Sage, Seer) *Patanjali* defines *Yoga* as *ChittVrittiNirodh* in the 2nd verse of Chapter I of his Text, *PatanjaliYogaSutras*. *Chitt* means attention, *Vritti* means its core essence, so, *ChittVritti* means the core essence of attention. *Nirodh* means the process of bringing back towards its very source, that is, to THE SELF, to the Spirit.

Thus *Yoga* is the process of bringing the core essence of the attention back towards its very source, without closing it to the outside world. When the attention is brought back towards its source without closing it to outside world (that is, making it aware of both, one's self and outside object simultaneously) it becomes consciousness.

There are various states of Consciousness as shown in the Diagrams of States of Consciousness, and within the particular state there are degrees. Consciousness can be known and experienced inside us only by its taste. In ordinary man moments of consciousness are very rare: they occur in exceptional moments like in highly emotional states, in moments of danger or beauty, in very new and unexpected circumstances and situations etc. For information about the properties of various states of consciousness, please refer to the Diagram of Properties of Various States of Consciousness.

Patanjali divides this process of *Yoga*, that is, process of attaining the Consciousness into 8 *Angs* (divisions) according to the progressive level of evolution. Combined reading of the 4th Way and *PatanjaliYogaSutra* unfolds the following picture. Please refer to the Diagram of *Patanjali AstangYoga* and the 4th Way.

Yam and Niyam: Broadly it means good householder discipline and rules. This is work on the level of *World 96*, that is, work on oneself to make the false personality and false ego passive and less insistent.

Ashan: (Comfortable and still posture): In human organism there are two systems of body liquids, the blood and the lymph. The Nature has provided an inbuilt pump, i.e. heart, for circulation of blood within the whole body, but the Nature has not provided any such pump for circulation of lymph in the body. However, the circulation of the lymph is required in order to cleanse the body and dispose of poisons.

The circulation of the lymph in the body is achieved by our movements. Whether we want or not but our lymph make us move. We can experience this by trying to sit still for 15-20 minutes: the lymph will itch and make us move consciously or unconsciously, and thereby do its work of circulation!

The lymph is under the direct influence of the Moon, like the water of the Sea. The Moon's effect on the Sea water can be seen directly on full moon and new moon days in the form of tides. This way it is said that all our movements are controlled and governed by the Moon.

Such unconscious movement propelled by the Moon through the lymph is the cause of all our unconscious habits and *mechanicalness.* Fortunately, for us it is not compulsory to move unconsciously, if we try to move intentionally with awareness. This aspect is dealt with in detail by Rodney Collin in his book *Theory of Celestial Influence* (pages from 109 to 122), published by Shambhala, Boulder and London, 1984.

The meaning of the 4th Way concept of ***Creating Moon within oneself*** is to develop ability to move intentionally with awareness, and thereby controlling the unconscious habits and *mechanicalness.*

Patanjali shows the tool of *Ashan* for this. *Ashan* means to be able to sit in still but comfortable posture for a period. *Patanjali* says it can be achieved by (1) *PrayatnShaithilya:* that is, the effort of rightly relaxing by using negative half of King of Spades (using negative half of the Intellectual part of the Moving Centre means *resting* with King's full attention) and (2) *AnantSamapatiAbhyasam:* that is, continuous effort of doing things intentionally and consciously (that is, doing moving activities using positive half of King of Spades with full attention). Intentional moving activities, like intentional physical work, yoga or other exercises are very useful, if done with full attention. This is work on the level of *World 48.*

Sitting in a still but relaxed posture for 15-20 minutes a day can have very good effect on one's *feeling of rooted-ness,* and on one's physical well being too.

The aspect of rightly relaxing unnecessary muscular tension in the body and its effects has been dealt with in detail by P. D. Ouspensky in Chapter XVII of his book, *In Search of the Miraculous,* published by Harcourt, Inc. (San Diego, New York and London). Therein he suggests that one should start relaxing muscular tension with the muscles of the face and then proceed downward. Relaxing facial muscular tension has profound effect on our state.

It is very pertinent to note that planet's rotation on its own axis is considered as index of the development of that particular planet. All known planets except Mercury rotate on their own axis. The Moon also does not rotate on its axis. The Moon controls unconscious movements and habits of man, and Mercury has affinity with the general nature of man's expressions.

It seems that the fact of these both heavenly bodies not rotating on their axis has direct bearing on the fact that these two aspects of man's psyche (that is, unconscious movements and habits, and the general nature of one's expression) are very difficult to change, and so, one's ability to observe and work on these aspects is the index of one's being. It needs right knowledge and long work on oneself.

Pranayam: (Relaxed and stilled breathing): When one is in intentional relaxed state, the breathing also starts occurring in right way, and approach the state of wordless breath. *Patanjali* says when inhalation and exhalation becomes stilled and relaxed it is called *Pranayam.*

When the state of *Pranayam* (relaxed and stilled inhalation-exhalation) is achieved it makes the way for taking and absorbing Impressions (*Tanmatras*) and thereby creates conduciveness for initial stage of self-remembering. This is work on the level of *World 24.*

Pratyahar: (Absorbing back in): When one indulges in the sense objects in identified way, the finer energy produced within human organism (reflected in attention) flows out through sense object identification and one feels drained of energy.

But when one has achieved the state of *Pranayam* (relaxed and stilled inhalation-exhalation) and intentionally divides attention by bringing back attention towards oneself and keeping attention on outside sense objects intact simultaneously, one is doing *Pratyahar* (taking in the energy of fine Impressions - *Tanmatras).* This is work on the advanced level of *World 24* and initial level of *World 12.*

Dharna: (Focusing on Consciousness): In the moment, when one is able to divide attention with sense objects and taking in Impressions, that time one can make further effort of focusing consciousness without using functions (that is, without using 4 Lower Centres and sense objects), in other words, the efforts of being in and focusing on the consciousness itself.

This effort of being in and focusing on the consciousness itself is called *Dharna* by *Patanjali.* This is work on the level of *World 12.*

Dhyan: (Continuous Consciousness): As a result of the prolonged efforts of being in and focusing on the consciousness itself, when the consciousness become continuous and stilled, it is called *Dhyan* by *Patanjali* (*PatanjaliYogaSutra* Chapter III – 2). This is continuous and profound 3rd state of consciousness. This is work on the advanced level of *World 12.*

Samadhi: (Sublime and balanced Intelligence - entering in Higher Mental Centre): When the continuous 3rd state of consciousness becomes so profound and deep that there does not remain any sense of the self (*SwarupShunyamiv* – the death of Lower self, not just passivity of Lower self) that moment is called *SabijSamadhi* by *Patanjali* (*PatanjaliYogaSutra* Chapter III – 3). This is approaching and entering into the 4th state of consciousness, and is a work on initial level of *World 6.*

Saiyam: When all the above three (*Dharna, Dhyan* and *Samadhi*) are occurring and applied simultaneously, it is called *Saiyam.* In *PatanjaliYogaSutra* Chapter III – 15 to 49, he gives various keys for attaining miraculous abilities to do (*Siddhis)* by applying *Saiyam* on various subjects. This is the work on advance level of *World 6.*

Kaivalyam: In *PatanjaliYogaSutra* Chapter III – 50, he says that after attaining miraculous ability to do (*Siddhis)* when one remain no longer interested in those *Siddhis*, and dies to his Higher Self (*Siddhis)*, he approaches and eventually attains the state of *Kaivalyam (NirbijSamadhi*, that is, state of *Tathata, Tao)*, the Spirit state.

He gives clues and keys for attaining *Kaivalyam* in *PatanjaliYogaSutra* - Chapter IV, However, one can understand and practically apply the keys according to one's level of being only. This is the work on the level of *World 3.*

One can benefit a lot by rightly synthesizing ideas of *Patanjali Yoga Sutras* and the 4th Way. Right combination of the *practical-ness* (scientific approach) and the sense of scale and relativity of the 4th Way, and various tools and keys of *Patanjali Yoga Sutra* can be of great help to any journeyman on the path of evolution.

Summary of work (Sadhana) on various levels

World 96 This is False Personality (False Ego) level. Chief work on this level is to follow rules and discipline of a good householder.

World 48 This is True Personality level. Work starts for one who has developed Magnetic Centre (*Khap-Mumukshuta)* by accumulating and absorbing sufficient amount of Influence B within oneself.

Magnetic Centre means *Khap*, a kind of dissatisfaction about leading just ordinary day-to-day worldly life, and so, the deep desire for spiritual evolution.

On this level the chief work is to study and try to understand esoteric knowledge; study of attention, and trying to control and keep attention; self observation on the basis of right principles, understanding human machine with clear understanding of its different centres, and division of centres into parts, and observing one's own machine's working; knowing one's Body-type, Chief Feature (*Swabhav*) and Centre of Gravity;

Working on king of spade, controlling unnecessary movements, avoiding *formatory* thinking and self-indulgence; understanding Essence and personality, relation between knowledge and being; understanding one's own false personality (false ego), and recognising its working in oneself by taste, and trying to make it more and more passive and less insistent.

General understanding of attitude, study of one's attitude, knowing the matters for which positive attitude s required, and matters for which negative attitude is required, and trying to develop right attitude in general and about the work in particular is other important aspect of work at this level.

Observation of the fact about when one is not true to oneself, and trying to be true to oneself and learning to try to relax one's attention is also a important aspect of work on this level.

Base of work Understanding degrees of consciousness by taste, learning to try to be more conscious than one is in the moment, in other words, learning to remember oneself; learning to be present; collecting oneself, coming back to oneself, bringing *ChittVriti* (essence of attention) back towards oneself, and dividing attention again and again whenever possible throughout the day is the chief base for real work.

World 24 This is working on emotional centre and eventually working on the Essence. Purifying the King of Heart with the use of Work "I"s and utterance of Work "I"s in sequence is work on Essence. Studying and understanding one's likes and dislikes, interests, identifications, and negative emotions; and focusing more on one's likes, enjoying the process of living and the work (*Sadhana*) is important aspect of work at this level.

Other aspects of the work at this level are: understanding why it is required not to express negative emotions and finding reasons for not expressing it; understanding the efforts of non-identifying (*Vairagya)* in general; and developing ability of separation by clear observation and acceptance that negative emotion is circulating within one in the moment as a fact, without deceiving oneself, and without judging or condemning oneself for that by right attitude that negative emotions usually exist in everyone, and for that I need not judge myself, but I need to study it, and at least try not to express it.

World 12 Experiencing wordless breaths after utterance of Work "I"s in sequence is the initial experience of *World 12*.

Cooperation with the Conscience and transformation of negative emotions by non- identifying (*Vairagya)*, separation and understanding its causes is the aspect of work on world 12 level.

For transformation one need to make specific effort to remember oneself, and at the same time try to not identify with negative emotions, this both seems one but they both are separate efforts which should happen simultaneously in the moment: 1st conscious shock of remembering oneself, and 2nd conscious shock of non- identifying with negative emotions occurring simultaneously.

One need to allow the transformation to happen by being wordless and still, separate from it, in a self remembering state, without fighting with it, and without *trying* to transform it.

It is a kind of effortless effort, in the sense that one's ordinary self, personality is not making any effort; it is just standing still in submission.

Other important aspects of the work at this level are: learning not to allow emotional centre to do its usual things like reacting, resenting and judging (on mental level, it is not thinking too much, and trying to keep mind wordless); and learning to leave things on Influence C.

World 6 The work at this level is connected with the process of dying. Before dying, one needs to awaken as to nothingness of one's ordinary self. This is an effort to die to oneself. This needs more or less continuous 3rd state of consciousness and the transformation as a way of life.

Learning to be in "not-seeking-anything" state is one of the important aspects of the work (*Sadhana)* at this level.

Trying to, rather allowing the state to appear where one is observing things and doing things as if one does not exist at all, for example, as if one is not in this room and still seeing what is happening here is one of the aspects of work on dying. This can come only out of the understanding of this state, as to what it means not to exist.

Attracting better aspects of one's luck

Luck means inherent tendency in the *Essence* of attracting certain kind of events & things, and also of falling under certain kind of natural laws in course of one's life. Mechanically and unknowingly the inherited tendencies determines the course of one's life.

Human inner world (i.e. thinking, feeling & actions) is governed by various types (qualities) of inner energies, which attract corresponding outer situations & events in the course of one's life. The interplay of these various energies is like a flux, and it fluctuates moment to moment; one moment one energy is active inside, and the next moment the another energy is active.

The lowest & crudest energy (i.e. *World96* Energy) that works in human being is connected with negative impulses of hatred, depression, anger etc. When it is active in one, one tends to express whatever negative emotions & reactions one is feeling inside, and has no control over his behavior, and that time anything can happen with him. This crudest energy attracts & creates crime, depression & such many other destructive activities & events.

The 2nd higher level of Energy (i.e. *World48* Energy) is connected with intentional, practical and right thinking. This 2nd level of energy attracts & creates good civilized life, business success, good social stature etc.

The 3rd higher level of Energy (i.e. *World24* Energy) is connected with fine emotions, at home-ness, doing & enjoying the activity of one's like & excellence, and not brooding or worrying much about anything. This 3rd level of energy attracts & creates extra-ordinary excellence in particular area of life like art etc, relaxed & kind of fulfilled life, and what we generally call good-luck, that is, tendency to attract good things in life with ease.

The 4th higher level of Energy (i.e. *World12* Energy, perhaps the highest & finest energy human being can work with) manifests as sex energy in ordinary human being, but when transmuted (in highly evolved human being) it reflects as non-identification (i.e. spiritual detachment), intense overall *wordless* clarity about the thing in question, peace, un-imposed self-discipline, and spontaneous joy. This 4th level of energy produces what we call great & timeless work. Though, there is still higher & refined energy, but ordinary human being can not understand or deal with it.

Paradoxically the "Luck" is both predetermined & is also in the hands of human being; predetermined in the sense that it is inherent & very deep (sub-conscious) tendency and very difficult to break, and it is in the hands of human being in the sense that if one knows & understands this interplay of energies, by right & consistent efforts one can modify it little by little. However, as per the ancient wisdom one can not change certain aspect of one's life like birth, childhood grooming, physical characteristics, kind of person one would marry with, death, etc.

When one deeply understands this interplay of energies by one's own experience of life, and understands that everything has degrees, he starts becoming more & more conscious/aware, and little by little starts attracting better influences & impressions, and by that attracts better aspects of one's luck. However, this is a very long process, and needs right understanding & consistent right efforts.

One way of approaching & dealing with this issue could be by intentionally choosing, moment by moment, to make one-self fall under higher inner energies. It would create the possibility of attracting corresponding better aspects of one's luck. Rightly understanding and consistently practicing the following may bring one more near to the 3rd higher level of energy (i.e. *World24* Energy), and attract better aspects of one's luck:

> (1) Learn to live according to your inner-likes. Don't worry about what will happen; things will fall in place. This is Universal Law; deepen this trust inside more & more.
>
> (2) Learn to mind your own business, keep focus on your capabilities, and don't compare yourself with others.

(3) Simply remain vigilant not to believe & express (i.e. understand that it is not mandatory to believe it as true & express it) the emotion of revenge, doubt, depression or any other such king of negative emotion when it occurs inside. Learn not to focus much on negative emotions & negative things.

(4) Understand & feel that I am gifted with special extraordinary inner ability (in fact everyone is, it may be hidden & unexplored, find out yours), don't seek the approval of others for that, as your life itself has many times given enough verifications of this; trust and keep such verifications alive.

(5) Understand that there is no need to doubt other people & situations unnecessarily, learn to evoke the emotion of friendship inside and deal with people through love, and learn to leave the mean logic & its profit-loss apart.

(6) Develop the attitude of giving. Learn to evoke the emotion & inner state of *giving* by focusing more on intention of giving (i.e. by asking oneself, how can I give more?), rather than intention of profiting.

At the moment when the 3rd higher level of energy (i.e. *World24* Energy) is circulating & active inside one, that time rightly understanding and practicing the following may bring one more near to the 4th higher level of energy (i.e. *World12* Energy), and create the possibility of attracting still better aspects of one's luck:

> Learn to abandon your *doership,* make efforts and still leave things & results on the intelligence of *higher invisible influences* & THE ALMIGHTY. Learn to keep the Mind wordless, and the Heart non-reactive & non-judgmental. Let the *higher invisible influences* penetrate inside and unfold the wordless understanding.

What it means to be in the Present

To be in the Present moment means being right here, *seeing* & feeling afresh as if for the first time, without dwelling on psychological Past or the Future. The *Presence* (being in the Present) has degrees; sometimes one is more in the presence, sometimes less, and sometimes completely in the grip of psychological past or future.

Dwelling on the Past means *seeing* & feeling thing which are in front of one on the basis of accumulated psychological habits, past psychological memories & experiences (actually which had occurred as a result of dwelling on the past or future at that point of time). For example, when one see a person who has badly insulted & harmed him in the past, the psychological memory of past experience of insult will evoke in one the emotion & attitude of resentment, anger, etc, and will color one's quality of *seeing,* feeling & attitude in the moment. *Seeing* & feeling in the moment through the undercurrent of the accumulated past hurt-feelings, injustice, feeling of bad luck, etc, *is,* in fact, the dwelling on the past.

Dwelling on the Future means *seeing* & feeling the things which are in front of one on the basis of personal expectations, anxiety or fear about what will happen in the next moment (future). For example, the occurrence of an event, depending upon one's believed positive-ness or negative-ness of its outcome, will color one's quality of *seeing,* feeling & attitude in the moment.

When one gets the right guidance and starts understanding that the past psychological experiences that one has accumulated inside are not real (not real in the sense, it need not necessarily be so, and all that has happened has happened as a result of dwelling on the past or the future at that point of time), one starts realizing its meaninglessness & the meaninglessness of dwelling on it again and again. As this realization deepens, little by little it helps one to be separate from it and disregard the inside accumulated psychological past & future, when its actual effects pops up in the moment. Such separation from the effects of psychological past & future has degrees, sometimes it is less, and sometimes it is more.

When one is separate & detached from the actual pops up effects in the moment of such psychological past & future without condemning it, and is able not to act it out, that time one is in the 3rd state of consciousness (consciousness of inside activity of the self, i.e. self-consciousness).

By right & consistent efforts if one acquires the ability to be in more or less continuous 3rd state of consciousness, and if one get the right guidance, by specific efforts one experiences the glimpses of the state in which the self, which accumulates the psychological past & future inside, is dead, it does not exist. In other words, in those moments one *sees* & feels things as they actually are without any psychological color. Such moments when the self, accumulator of psychological past & future, is dead & does not exist, are the moments of 4th state of consciousness (Objective Consciousness).

Within the 3rd state of consciousness there are various degrees, and within the 4th state also there are various degrees. In this way, the state of *Presence* has various degrees.

If we try to understand this in terms of *Satva, Rajasa* & *Tamasa,* in effect it means, being in the Present is being in *Satva,* being in the psychological past is being in *Tamasa,* and being in psychological future is being in *Rajasa* (i.e. the sense of doership in view of acquiring something in *future,* and all the momentum coming out of that sense & desire). We can see that the consistent work on all the three is required for the right results.

Eastern Astro-Science

Here we are using the term Eastern Astro-Science to mean that ancient science which deals with the man's psychological constitution as to on what it depend, how it is connected with higher cosmoses, how higher cosmoses of planets affect it, how man is a miniature cosmos containing everything that exist in progressively higher cosmoses, how it is ***as above as below***, how the same universal laws apply to man as well as to higher cosmoses of planets etc., and how one's psychological constitution can be altered to make the spiritual evolution a real possibility for one; as against the Astrology, which is ordinarily understood to be dealing with predictions of events in man's life on the basis of movements of planets. Here the ordinary Astrology is not our concern or interest.

Law of Fate (Law of Types)

Accumulated effects of past Actions, if done consistently, enters into the Essence (Causal body) and becomes very nature of it, and reflects as its permanent tendencies, like one's Body-Type, which is embedded into one's Essence so much so that it has became one with it. Such permanent tendencies are very difficult to alter; and it attracts as well as creates the Law of Fate for one. If one develops Magnetic Centre (*Khap-Mumukshuta*) and does efforts for evolution consistently, one acquires permanent tendency to evolve and it becomes part of one's Essence (Causal body), and forms part of one's fate and which goes with one from life to life.

Law of Will (Inner)

As in everything, at this level of evolution also there are degrees, but at the highest degree of evolution at this level, one has Self-consciousness (3rd State) to observe and witness one's Chief Feature and *mechanicality*, and has intentional decision not to operate from the Chief Feature and has enough Self-remembrance and unity to carry out that decision.

This results into ability of Non-doing the Chief Feature, which amounts to actualisation of one's one chief possibility, i.e. Ability to do one's Body-type Activity in its highest and purest form. In the basic triad working at this level the Self-consciousness is the 3rd force, Will is the 1st force, and Unity is the 2nd force.

Law of Will (Inner and Outer)

As in everything, at this level of evolution also there are degrees, but at the highest degree of evolution at this level, one has Objective consciousness (4th State), all possible objective knowledge, *SatyaSankalp* (conscious wish), and miraculous ability to do (*Siddhis)*. One has realised all the possibilities one has in one's Essence (Causal body). One is law unto oneself within our solar system. One has purified all three forces (*Satva-Rajasa-Tamasa*) to the utmost degree, and so, one has control over all six processes. One can do anything one wishes, one has *Vachansiddhi* (one's words turns into facts). One is *Siddh*, and as natural consequence of the depth and profoundness of one's being one has many unknown *Siddhis* (miraculous abilities).

In the basic triad working at this level the Objective consciousness (*PurnGyanShakti*) is the 3rd force, Conscious wish (*SatyaSankalp*) is the 1st force, and miraculous ability to do (*PurnKaryaShakti*) is the 2nd force.

Kaivalya - Tathata – Tao

When one has attained miraculous ability to do (Higher Centres and *Siddhis*), and if one realises that operating from *Siddhis* is obstacle for further development of one's being. then possibility of *Kaivalya* comes into being. The term *Kaivalya* (or *Keval Gyan*) is used in Jainism, *Tathata* is used in Buddhism, *Kaivalyam* is used by *Patanjali,* and Tao is used by Laotzu, all four speaks about more or less the same thing at the same level, though in different ways and words.

At this level of evolution, one has created and fulfilled the new possibilities of no-mind, *Kaivalya, Tathata, Tao, Akarma*, and ability of non-doing *Siddhis,* non-doing higher self.

To grasp the meaning of this we need to use one allegory of comparing animals, ordinary man and highly evolved man. Animals don't have ability to think, but we human beings have the ability to think, i.e. we are more evolved than animals. In the same way, Man No 1,2,3 and 4s do not have Higher Emotional and Higher Mental Centres as like the animals do not have man's ordinary thinking mind, i.e. man having Higher Centres are more evolved than ordinary man.

We all have, at some point of time, experienced that when our ordinary mind is not thinking, not chattering inside, and is wordless; and our heart is not resenting and judging anything, and is just standing still in aliveness, for us it is moments of bliss. At such moments our potential ability of not allowing our ordinary mind and heart to do its usual activity has manifested for few moments, giving us tremendous peace and bliss.

Now we can try to understand the same phenomena in connection with highly evolved man: if in those moments when we have ability not to allow our ordinary mind and heart to do its usual activity, we have such a bliss and peace, then what amount of bliss, peace and profoundness of being one might be having when one has moments when one is able not to allow his Higher Centres (Higher Minds) to do its usual activities (Higher Centres' usual activities are miraculous ability to do, *Siddhis* etc)!

If one realises the above, and decides not to operate from *Siddhis* and Higher Centres, and lets the Grand Scheme (for atheist it is Scheme of Creation and for theist it is Scheme of THE ALMIGHTY) prevail, and flows with the Grand Scheme in bliss of *Keval Gyan*. This makes one eventually to attain the State of *Kaivalya* (*Tathata -Tao*).

At the highest degree of evolution of this level, one is in *no-mind* state in its true sense, one is completely freed from Causal body, and therefore, it is *Kaivalya* state (i.e. nothing other than Spirit and its bliss).

For an atheist it is experiencing oneself as THAT, and that there is nothing beyond I AM THAT state. (This is ultimate Si-Do interval in the ultimate Ascending Octave).

For a theist it is experiencing oneself as Spirit (*Atman*), and one abandons fruits of one's actions completely, one devotes all his actions to HIM. (In the Bhagwad Geeta – IV (16 to 24), the description of this state is given in more detail).

Anadi (uncreated) *Panch Maha Bheda* (5 Entities)

According to Hindu Texts *Jiva* (un-evolved Spirit), *Ishwara* (Greater Beings - *World 3*s, *World 6*s and *World 12*s), Maya (the whole web of laws governing the Universe), *AksharBrahm* and *ParamBrahm* are *PanchMahaBheda*, that is, 5 ever existing (not created, without beginning and without end - *Anadi*) Entities.

Jivas and *Ishwaras* go into respective oblivion on respective Destruction (*Pralaya*), and again manifest on Creation. They both need to transcend Maya wholly to attain *Brahmi* State.

To grasp the meaning of world *Anadi*, we need to take one allegory. Suppose, if we destroy a ten storey building, then what would remain there? The answer is, there will remain open space in place of that destroyed building. If the entire city in which that building is situated is somehow destroyed, then what would remain there? Again the answer is the open space. Suppose, if the entire Earth is somehow destroyed, then what would remain in place of destroyed Earth? Again the answer is the space. Now suppose, if the Sun, the Milky Way, all other known and unknown galaxies, the entire Universe is somehow destroyed, then what will remain there?

As per Hindu Texts everything that exists, comes from and goes back into the Space (However, there is various grades of Space as per it purity and the Cosmic Level, explained in explanatory note "Quality of various orders of Space). On Atyantic Pralaya (Total Destruction) the entire Existence, the basic quantum (particle) of matter, and the time, the passage of which keeps the entire Universe in Existence will shrink into Non-existence (Oblivion - singularity); the life principle will also go in Oblivion state in that Non-existence.

That which is beyond, and source of, Existence and Non-existence both is called *Chidakash* or *AksharBrahm*.

For us it is unfathomable that how can anything be beyond Existence and Non-existence both. We can try to understand it in this way: the Existence means the state in which things are in its manifest form and exists in time. The Non-existence (Oblivion) means the state in which things are in un-manifest (i.e. seed form) and the time have totally ceased to exist, like the death at human level.

Chidakash or *AksharBrahm* is beyond both, and cause for the both, and being beyond the both it is imperishable, we may say that it is the *alive illumined nothingness.*

ParamBrahm, THE ALMIGHTY, is the Entity, who initiates Creation and Destruction. (In the Bhagwad Geeta – XV the characteristics of *ParmBrahm,* THE ALMIGHTY, are described, particularly in verse 18).

On *Atyantic Pralaya* (Total Destruction) the basic principle of *Maya* shrinks in the form of seed into the Non-existence (Oblivion), and on Creation again comes into being and it itself proceeds to create various levels of *Worlds.* On *Pralaya* the life principle of *Jivas* and *Ishwaras* also shrinks in the form of seed into the Non-existence (Oblivion), and on Creation again manifest according to their respective level of being.

As per the Hindu Texts (Bhagwan Swaminarayan's *Vachnamrit Gadhada* I-8), no one has created *Jivas, Ishwaras, Maya, AksharBrahm* and *ParmBrahm*; they were, they are, and they will always be - this is the meaning of *Anadi.*

Sublime Ascent of the Soul

In first part of his poem "Sublime Ascent of the Soul" Rumi celebrates himself for his evolution from mineral state to the state of being born as man. This realization of his own evolution gave him sound basis for having unwavering faith in still better possibilities lying ahead.

In the second part of this poem Rumi says that when one dies as mean and ordinary psychological self (Lower self), and is reborn, becomes enlightened (that is, the angelic qualities of unconditional love, compassion, child-like pure godly wisdom, etc becomes his very nature), one soars with angels blessed.

But, then, he says that except the Absolute (*Akshar-Brahm*), such relative immortality (existence after death as angel or god) comes to an end at some point of time, however inconceivably long may be such existence in angelic self.

In the third part of this poem, after realizing mortality of the relative immortality Rumi says when I have sacrificed my angel Soul (the sense of oneness with angel Soul) and be *fana* in HIM, then I shall experience the state, which no mind (not even the highest mind of angel Soul) can fathom.

To be *fana* means to die to one's angel Soul (letting go of the sense of oneness with the Higher Self) for being in *Brahmic* devotion towards the beyond-ness and the GLORY of THE ALMIGHTY. And he exclaims "Oh, let me not exist" i.e. let me die to my Higher Self. For his such Non Existence state (*fana*-state or *Brahmi* state) proclaims "To HIM we shall return".

When one has fully actualised one's All Possibilities (including new possibilities created) and has attained the State of *Kaivalya;* and if he has the grace and guidance of Man No. 9 and realises that the GRAND GRORY of *ParamBrahm*, THE ALMIGHTY is still far far beyond, and no evolution can attain HIS State, and the extent of HIS beyond-ness can not be fathomed by any mind; then only the true *fana* in *Brahmic* devotion for HIM takes place in his being, which along with the grace of THE ALMIGHTY, makes one to eventually attain the *Brahmi* state.

Only at this level of evolution one attains the eligibility to be *fana* in *Brahmic* devotion towards *ParamBrahm*, THE ALMIGHTY, till then the quality of one's devotion is relative, and is according to one's level of being, and so, can not fully reach *ParamBrahm*, THE ALMIGHTY. In the Bhagwad Geeta – VIII the psychological aspect of *AksharBrahm* (the Absolute) is described, particularly in verses 3, 20, 21 and 22.

Quality of Devotion *(Bhakti)* at various levels of being

Quality of one's devotion (if one has) for THE ALMIGHTY depends on one's level of being. Devotion of Man No. 1, 2 or 3 is usually consist of performing religious rituals, blind faith without understanding, and having religious and philosophical dogmas.

The Devotion of Man No. 4 is based on valuation and understanding of evolution derived by relatively balanced thought, emotion and impulse; and is for seeking the help, guidance and grace of THE ALMIGHTY, according to his subjective understanding of THE ALMIGHTY.

The Devotion of Man No. 5 is of the quality of 3rd state of consciousness, that is, after transcending the Lower self, but the Lower self still exist passively as undercurrent. The Devotion of Man No. 6 is of the quality of initial degree of 4th state of consciousness (that is, it is with *Uttam Savikalp Nischay)* and is at the very threshold of the death of the Lower self. The Devotion of Man No. 7 is of the quality of advanced degree of 4th state of consciousness, and after the death of the Lower self, and so it is most pure and self less in true sense. The Devotion of Man

No. 8 is after the death of the Higher Self (that is, it is with *UttamNirvikapNischay*). At present the Devotion of Man No. 8 is beyond our fathoming capacity.

As the understanding of THE ALMIGHTY and the Devotion for HIM is according to one's level of being, only Man No. 9 has *Complete and Right* understanding of THE ALMIGHTY, and so, has the highest quality of Devotion for HIM.

As like, Man No. 1, 2, 3 or 4 may or may not have the Devotion for and Belief in THE ALMIGHTY, in the same way Man No. 5, or Man No. 6, or Man No.7, or Man No. 8 may or may not have Belief in and Devotion for THE ALMIGHTY. However, the fact of having Belief in and Devotion for THE ALMIGHTY has profound effect on one' evolution, but one can come to understand this over a time only. Moreover, without having the Belief in and Devotion for THE ALMIGHTY, no one can evolve to the level of Man No. 9.

Section IV: Summary

Relativity of various Paths of Evolution

The 4th Way as expounded by G. I. Gurdjieff, P. D. Ouspensky and Rodney Collin, if rightly understood, imparts the knowledge necessary for attaining the spiritual evolution upto the level of Man No. 7. In the known 4th Way texts the possibility of evolution beyond Man No. 7 is not conceived, and moreover, there is no direction or theory beyond that point.

But, most importantly the scientific approach, practical understanding and searchlight of the Law of three and the Principle of Scale and Relativity of the 4th Way is fundamental key for anyone who wishes to evolve.

The Path of Buddhism and Jainism, if rightly understood, impart the knowledge necessary for attaining the spiritual evolution upto the level of Man No.8. In their known texts the possibility of evolution beyond Man No. 8 (*Kaivalya, Tathata, Tao*) is not conceived, and moreover, there is no direction or theory beyond that point.

The Path of Hinduism and Sufism, if rightly understood, impart the knowledge necessary for attaining the spiritual evolution upto the level of Man No. 9. As for the Sufism, we have seen in the above poem the urge of Rumi (a sufi) for returning to HIM, abandoning the bliss of Higher Self, and even abandoning the absolute freedom of the Spirit. And as for the Hinduism, combine reading of *Mandukya Upnishad* and the Bhagwad Geeta, particularly its Chapter 8 (*Akshar Brahm*), Chapter 12 (*Bhakti Yoga*) and Chapter 15 (*Purushottam*), show this possibility, direction and the theory for attaining it.

But, for one, without the *Practical-ness* of the 4th Way, the right understanding of scale and relativity and the right guidance and grace, the higher esoteric teachings like *Vedanta, Kaivalya, Tathata, Tao, Akshar Brahm* etc. may remain mere philosophy or dogma only.

So, it is not the question of one Path is better than the other. But, the synthesis of all the Paths together with right sense of Scale & Relativity gives one more clear & focused direction for the evolution. In the 4th Way the focus is more on practical-ness, scientific approach & primary necessity of realising one's actual present place, and then beginning from there. In the esoteric teachings of Jainism, Buddhism & Tao the focus is more on understanding & actualising of one's highest potential, which is, attaining the supreme freedom & bliss of the Spirit state. In the esoteric teachings of Hinduism & Sufism the focus is more on attaining the Spirit state and simultaneously serving THE ALMIGHTY, that is,

Brahmrup Devotion (sublime *Fana*) for *ParamBrahm*, THE ALMIGHTY, THE ALLAH.

Importance of the clarity & correctness of one's Road-map

Clear & correct Road-map is pre-requisite of any meaningful journey. If one has no clarity about the *Whole*, and do not have the clear & correct Road-map of his journey, it becomes the chief blockage in one's way over a period of time.

For example, if one comes to believe from his teacher & by his personal subjective study that the Lower self, which accumulates psychological past & future inside, can not be made to die and will always remain as undercurrent producing various "I"s & negative emotions, and that to be separate from it is all that there is, then one can not understand the 4th state of consciousness, as his Road-map ends here, and hence his journey, if proceed at all, will ends at the 3rd state of consciousness.

If one comes to believe from his teacher & by his personal study that the death of the Lower self, and acquiring the miraculous power and ability to do of the 4th state of consciousness, and that acquiring the Higher Self is all that there is, then one can not understand the Spirit State –*Atmabhav,* as his Road-map ends here, and hence his journey, if proceed, will end at the 4th state of consciousness.

(According to the Hindu Texts, particularly Chapter IV of The *Patanjal YogSutra*, the *AtmaBhav,* the *Kaivalyam* comes into being as a result of the death of the Higher Self by acquiring *Vairagy* – indifference – towards the miraculous powers of the Higher Self)

If one comes to believe from his teacher & by his personal study that the death of the Higher Self and acquiring the Spirit State –Atmabhav is all that there is, then one can not understand the Brahmi State - Brahmbhav, as his Road-map ends here, and hence his journey, if proceed, will end at the Spirit State –Atmabhav. This is ultimate Si-Do Interval in the overall Octave of Evolution.

(According to the Hindu Texts, particularly Chapter VIII, XII & XV of The Bhagwad Geeta, *Brahmi* State comes into being as a result of the death of one's Higher Self, and realizing that the Supreme Self of *ParamBrahm,* THE ALMIGHTY, THE ALLAH is beyond everyone, no one can reach HIS BEING, and realizing this if one bows down to HIM and serves HIM)

The Greatest Luck

Having sound Magnetic Centre (*Khap-Mumukshuta*) and right valuation for evolution; having opportunity to co-work (co-*Sadhana*) with Man No. 4s or 5; having grace to work under the guidance of Man No. 6 or 7; and having sublime grace of meeting Man No. 8 or 9, truly recognising him by characteristics for what he is, valuing, trusting and serving him above all, and having his grace; is the greatest possible luck a man can have.

To understand it by an allegory, suppose two boys of the same caliber and same family background are studying in the same school in the same class. One of the boys has somehow opportunity to do in critical moments something very good and very personal for Mr. A, a billionaire (or say, the Sovereign King) and that happy billionaire adopts that boy as his son.

We can visualise the difference that will come about in the life of adopted boy compared to the life of another boy, even though the adopted boy may not understand the full implications of his adoption (over a period he would come to understand it), but still he has full benefit of his adoption by the billionaire.

Meeting and recognising Man No. 8 or 9, having love for him, and earning his good wishes and grace is like the adoption by the billionaire as in our above allegory; such is the unexplainable beauty of the love for and the grace of Man No. 8 or Man No.9.

However, such luck and opportunity is very rare, and one can not afford to wait for it. One has to take control of one's life and make right and consistent efforts for evolution on right basis.

The Summary in nutshell

We can understand this entire process in nutshell by taking an allegory of a Lamp. The Lamp itself, a source from which the light spreads, is *Atman* (Spirit); the Power Current illuminating the Lamp is *Akshar Brahm* (the Absolute); the owner and the supplier of the Power Current is *Param Brahm,* THE ALMIGHTY.

The light that spreads from the Lamp is the Consciousness: as one's level of being descends the state of consciousness also descends, closer to *Atman* (Spirit) is 4th state of Consciousness, next is 3rd state of Consciousness, like as one moves away from the Lamp, the quality and density of the Light reduces. The Lamp's visibility from afar without its actual Light is the state of controlled and directed Attention;

and the utter darkness due to so much distance from the Lamp that the Lamp itself is not visible is the state of wondering or no attention.

So, our *Journey within* is from the state of controlled and directed Attention (where we are at present, or can be at any moment we intend) to *Atman* (the Spirit), and serving THE ALMIGHTY. In other words, our journey is from afar to nearer, and then to be established right into *Atman* (the Spirit), and serving THE ALMIGHTY.

This Sweet Unrest

I wonder! Is this work an objective thought?
Mr. "I" does wish that it be acclaimed,
But, who knows how in my mind it was brought.
And who'll believe that it's worthy to be famed?

So, fearing scorn from friends, I used to say,
"I've read an Idea and liked it much,
Would you too like to read it, by the way,
And tell me, does deeply the Soul it touch?"

But, when I dared to lay it at thy feet
Thou, with thy taintless and grace flowing eyes,
Lovedst it. Ah, what a wondrous tryst
It was! This flood of bliss may break the skies!

My Muse has served the purpose at her best,
As thou art with me in this sweet unrest!

Appendix: Mandukya Upnishad

Mandukya Upnishad is considered as one of 10 most important *Upnishads* in entire *Vedanta* Texts. It is a small *Upnishad* containing 12 verses. The 1st verse explains about the physical being of the Absolute. In verses from 2 to 8, psychological aspect of various worlds from ***World 12*** to ***World 1*** is explained, and in last 4 verses characteristics of states of consciousness of various worlds from ***World 12*** to ***World 1*** is explained. Following is the original Sanskrit Verses along with author's translation of it in English.

माण्डूक्योपनिषद् (Mandukya Upanishad)

शान्तिपाठ

ॐ भद्रं कर्णेभिः शृणुयाम देवा भद्रं पश्येमाक्षभिर्यजत्राः ।
स्थिरैरङ्गैस्तुष्टुवाँसस्तनूभिर्व्यशेम देवहितं यदायुः ॥
स्वस्ति न इन्द्रो वृद्धश्रवाः स्वस्ति नः पूषा विश्ववेदाः॥
स्वस्ति नस्ताक्ष्यो अरिष्टनेमिः स्वस्ति नो बृहस्पतिर्दधातु ॥

ॐ शान्तिः ! शान्तिः !! शान्तिः !!!

Peace Invocation

Om. Shining Ones! May we hear through our ears what is auspicious. Ye, fit to be worshipped ! May we see with our eyes what is auspicious. May we, endowed with body strong with limbs, offering praise, complete the full span of life bestowed upon us by the divine beings. May Indra, of enhanced fame, be auspicious unto us. May Pushan, who is all-knowing, be auspicious unto us. May Tarkshya, who is the destroyer of all evils, be auspicious unto us. May Brihaspati bestow upon us auspiciousness!

Om Peace ! Peace! Peace !

1 ओमित्येतदक्षरमिदँ सर्वं तस्योपव्याख्यानं भूतं भवद्भविष्यदिति सर्वमोङ्कार
एव । यच्चान्यत् त्रिकालातीतं तदप्योङ्कार एव ॥

OM ! - This Imperishable Word is the whole of this visible universe. Its explanation is as follows: What has become, what is becoming, what will become, - verily, all of this is OM. And what is beyond these three states of the world of time, - that too, verily, is OM.

2 सर्वँ ह्येतद् ब्रह्मायमात्मा ब्रह्म सोऽयमात्मा चतुष्पात् ॥

All this, verily, is Brahman. The Self is Brahman. This Self has four quarters.

3. जागरितस्थानो बहिष्प्रज्ञः सप्ताङ्ग एकोनविंशतिमुखः स्थूलभुग्वैश्वानरः प्रथमः पादः ॥

The first quarter is Vaisvanara. Its field is the waking state. Its consciousness is outward-turned. It is seven-limbed and nineteen-mouthed. It enjoys gross objects.

4. स्वप्नस्थानोऽन्तःप्रज्ञः सप्ताङ्ग एकोनविंशतिमुखः प्रविविक्तभुक् तैजसो द्वितीयः पादः ॥

The second quarter is Taijasa. Its field is the dream state. Its consciousness is inward-turned. It is seven-limbed and nineteen-mouthed. It enjoys subtle objects.

5. यत्र सुप्तो न कञ्चन कामं कामयते न कञ्चन स्वप्नं पश्यति तत्सुषुप्तम् । सुषुप्तस्थान एकीभूतः प्रज्ञानघन एवानन्दमयो ह्यानन्दभुक्चेतोमुखः प्राज्ञस्तृतीयः पादः ॥

The third quarter is Prajna, where one asleep neither desires anything nor beholds any dream: that is deep sleep. In this field of dreamless sleep, one becomes undivided, an undifferentiated mass of consciousness, consisting of bliss and feeding on bliss. His mouth is consciousness.

6. एष सर्वेश्वर एक सर्वज्ञ एषोऽन्तर्याम्येष योनिः सर्वस्य प्रभावप्ययौ हि भूतानाम् ॥६॥

This is the Lord of All; the Omniscient; the Indwelling Controller; the Source of All. This is the beginning and end of all beings.

7. नान्तःप्रज्ञं न बहिष्प्रज्ञं नोभयतः प्रज्ञं न प्रज्ञानघनं न प्रज्ञं नाप्रज्ञम् । अदृष्टमव्यवहार्यमग्राह्यमलक्षणमचिन्त्यमव्यपदेश्यमेकात्मप्रत्ययसारं प्रपञ्चोपशमं शान्तं शिवमद्वैतं चतुर्थं मन्यन्ते स आत्मा स विज्ञेयः ॥

That is known as the fourth quarter: neither inward-turned nor outwardturned consciousness, nor the two together; not an indifferentiated mass of consciousness; neither knowing, nor unknowing; invisible, ineffable, intangible, devoid of characteristics, inconceivable, indefinable, its sole essence being the consciousness of its own Self; the coming to rest of all relative existence; utterly quiet; peaceful; blissful: without a second: this is the Atman, the Self; this is to be realised.

8. सोऽयमात्माध्यक्षरमोङ्कारोऽधिमात्रं पादा मात्रा मात्राश्च पादा अकार उकारो मकार इति ॥

This identical Atman, or Self, in the realm of sound is the syllable OM, the above described four quarters of the Self being identical with the components of the syllable, and the components of the syllable being identical with the four quarters of the Self. The components of the Syllable are A, U, M.

9. जागरितस्थानो वैश्वानरोऽकारः प्रथमा मात्राऽऽप्तेरादिमत्त्वाद्वाऽऽप्नोति ह वै सर्वान्कामानादिश्च भवति य एवं वेद ॥

Vaisvanara, whose field is the waking state, is the first sound, A, because this encompasses all, and because it is the first. He who knows (witnesses) thus, encompasses all desirable objects; he becomes the first.

10. स्वप्नस्थानस्तैजस उकारो द्वितीया मात्रोत्कर्षादुभयत्वाद्वोत्कर्षति ह वै ज्ञानसंततिं समानश्च भवति नास्याब्रह्मवित्कुले भवति य एवं वेद ॥

Taijasa, whose field is the dream state, is the second sound, U, because this is an excellence, and contains the qualities of the other two. He who knows (witnesses) thus, exalts the flow of knowledge and becomes equalised; in his family there will be born no one ignorant of Brahman.

11. सुषुप्तस्थान : प्राज्ञो मकारस्तृतीया मात्रा मितेरपीतेर्वा मिनोति ह वा इदं सर्वमपीतिश्च भवति य एवं वेद ॥

Prajna, whose field is deep sleep, is the third sound, M, because this is the measure, and that into which all enters. He who knows (witnesses) thus, measures all and becomes all.

12. अमात्रश्चतुर्थोऽव्यवहार्यः प्रपञ्चोपशमः शिवोऽद्वैत एवमोङ्कार आत्मैव संविशत्यात्मनाऽऽत्मानं य एवं वेद य एवं वेद ॥

The fourth is soundless: unutterable, a quieting down of all relative manifestations, blissful, peaceful, non-dual. Thus, OM is the Atman, verily. He who knows (experiences) thus, merges his self in the Self; - year, he who knows (experiences) thus.

Om Peace! Peace! Peace!

शान्तिपाठ

ॐ भद्रं कर्णेभिः शृणुयाम देवा भद्रं पश्येमाक्षभिर्यजत्राः ।
स्थिरैरङ्गैस्तुष्टुवा ँसस्तनूभिर्व्यशेम देवहितं यदायुः ॥
स्वस्ति न इन्द्रो वृद्धश्रवाः स्वस्ति नः पूषा विश्ववेदाः॥
स्वस्ति नस्ताक्ष्र्यो अरिष्टनेमिः स्वस्ति नो बृहस्पतिर्दधातु ॥
ॐ शान्तिः ! शान्तिः !! शान्तिः !!!

Peace Invocation

Aum Bhadram Karnebhihi Shrunuyaama
Deva Bhadram Pashyemaksha Bhirya Jatraha |
Sthirai Rangaisthustuvasatanubhihi Vyasheema
Devagitam Adaayuhu ||
Swasti Na Indro Vriddhashrava Swasti Na Pusha
Vishwavedha |
Swasti Nastarkshyo Arishta Nemihi Swasti
Nobhrihaspatirdhaatu ||

Aum Shanti ! Shanti ! Shanti !

List of Diagrams & Enneagrams

1. Diagrams

2 Enneagrams

Bibliography

G. I. Gurdjieff:
Beelzebub's Tales to his Grandson
Meeting with Remarkable Men
Life is Real only then, when "I AM"
Views from the Real World

P. D. Ouspensky
In the Search of the Miraculous
The Psychology of Man's Possible Evolution
The Fourth Way

Rodney Collin: The Theory of Celestial Influence

Robert Earl Burton: Self Remembering

The Philokalia

The Works of William Shakespeare

Susan Zannos: Human Types: Essence and the Enneagram

J. Krishnamurti: The First and Last Freedom

Rabindranath Tagore: Gitanjali

Dada Bhagwan: Works of Dada Bhagwan (*AptVani)*

Hafiz: Poetry

Kabir: Poetry

Lao Tzu: Tao Te Ching

Shri Ramana Maharshi: Who Am I

Buddha (Buddhist Texts)

Maharshi Patanjali: *Patanjali Yoga Sutras*

Rumi: Poetry

Mandukya Upnisad – (A *Vedantic* Text)

The Bhagwad Geeta

Bhagwan Shri Swaminarayan: *Vachnamrits*

CPSIA information can be obtained at www.ICGtesting.com
Printed in the USA
LVOW11s1400251115

464193LV00004B/285/P